Boston College

Boston, Massachusetts

Written by Kelley Gossett

Edited by Adam Burns, Kimberly Moore, and Carrie Petersen

Layout by Jon Skindzier

Additional contributions by Omid Gohari, Christina Koshzow, Chris Mason, Joey Rahimi, and Luke Skurman

ISBN # 1-4274-0023-7
ISSN # 1551-9538
© Copyright 2006 College Prowler
All Rights Reserved
Printed in the U.S.A.
www.collegeprowler.com

Last updated 5/15/06

Special Thanks To: Babs Carryer, Andy Hannah, LaunchCyte, Tim O'Brien, Bob Sehlinger, Thomas Emerson, Andrew Skurman, Barbara Skurman, Bert Mann, Dave Lehman, Daniel Fayock, Chris Babyak, The Donald H. Jones Center for Entrepreneurship, Terry Slease, Jerry McGinnis, Bill Ecenberger, Idie McGinty, Kyle Russell, Jacque Zaremba, Larry Winderbaum, Roland Allen, Jon Reider, Team Evankovich, Lauren Varacalli, Abu Noaman, Mark Exler, Daniel Steinmeyer, Jared Cohon, Gabriela Oates, David Koegler, and Glen Meakem.

Bounce-Back Team: Amy Gallo, Cristina Tudino, and Nolan Kelly.

College Prowler®
5001 Baum Blvd.
Suite 750
Pittsburgh, PA 15213

Phone: 1-800-290-2682
Fax: 1-800-772-4972
E-Mail: info@collegeprowler.com
Web Site: www.collegeprowler.com

Welcome to College Prowler®

During the writing of College Prowler's guidebooks, we felt it was critical that our content was unbiased and unaffiliated with any college or university. We think it's important that our readers get honest information and a realistic impression of the student opinions on any campus—that's why if any aspect of a particular school is terrible, we (unlike a campus brochure) intend to publish it. While we do keep an eye out for the occasional extremist—the cheerleader or the cynic—we take pride in letting the students tell it like it is. We strive to create a book that's as representative as possible of each particular campus. Our books cover both the good and the bad, and whether the survey responses point to recurring trends or a variation in opinion, these sentiments are directly and proportionally expressed through our guides.

College Prowler guidebooks are in the hands of students throughout the entire process of their creation. Because you can't make student-written guides without the students, we have students at each campus who help write, randomly survey their peers, edit, layout, and perform accuracy checks on every book that we publish. From the very beginning, student writers gather the most up-to-date stats, facts, and inside information on their colleges. They fill each section with student quotes and summarize the findings in editorial reviews. In addition, each school receives a collection of letter grades (A through F) that reflect student opinion and help to represent contentment, prominence, or satisfaction for each of our 20 specific categories. Just as in grade school, the higher the mark the more content, more prominent, or more satisfied the students are with the particular category.

Once a book is written, additional students serve as editors and check for accuracy even more extensively. Our bounce-back team—a group of randomly selected students who have no involvement with the project—are asked to read over the material in order to help ensure that the book accurately expresses every aspect of the university and its students. This same process is applied to the 200-plus schools College Prowler currently covers. Each book is the result of endless student contributions, hundreds of pages of research and writing, and countless hours of hard work. All of this has led to the creation of a student information network that stretches across the nation to every school that we cover. It's no easy accomplishment, but it's the reason that our guides are such a great resource.

When reading our books and looking at our grades, keep in mind that every college is different and that the students who make up each school are not uniform—as a result, it is important to assess schools on a case-by-case basis. Because it's impossible to summarize an entire school with a single number or description, each book provides a dialogue, not a decision, that's made up of 20 different topics and hundreds of student quotes. In the end, we hope that this guide will serve as a valuable tool in your college selection process. Enjoy!

OMID GOHARI ◯ CHRISTINA KOSHZOW ◯ CHRIS MASON ◯ JOEY RAHIMI ◯ LUKE SKURMAN ◯
The College Prowler Team

Table of Contents

Introduction from the Author

Initially, I didn't like Boston College. My problem was that I arrived on campus freshman year with unreasonable expectations about my college career and my university. I somehow believed that I would instantly become best friends not only with my roommate, but with every other fascinating individual in my adorable and spacious dorm. My classes would be with an eclectic mix of students from all walks of life, and the lectures would be so intriguing that I would barely even need to study. Furthermore, my social life would be wild and crazy, with my amazingly easy entry into the local pubs thanks to the fake ID I would miraculously find laying in the street. The days would fly by with joy and ease. They would be punctuated by student rallies, tailgates, and deep coffee shop conversations with a hunky foreigner named Sven. I would also meet the love of my life and start planning our wedding sometime during second semester.

Obviously, I entered Chestnut Hill expecting the Hollywood version of college life. The truth is that there are more people at BC from the same background than I'd anticipated. Best friendships didn't spring up all over the place, although I did get very lucky in that department. Classes were definitely challenging, and I actually needed to spend long hours at the library to earn good grades. Also, it was certainly an uphill battle trying to maintain a boisterous social life while still underage. Nevertheless, once the initial shock dissipated, I began to see how much there is to appreciate at Boston College. I know now that BC delivered an important lesson early on: happiness doesn't just automatically happen, and re-evaluating your priorities and adjusting to your surroundings is a mandatory survival skill for any college student, no matter the school.

I recently graduated from BC, and in the end, it was the best school for me to attend. I received the most incredible education and made fantastic friends. I loved my time at BC and I urge all prospective students to read this book and see if BC is what you're really looking for in a college.

Kelley Gossett, Author
Boston College

By the Numbers

General Information

Boston College
140 Commonwealth Ave.
Chestnut Hill, MA 02467

Control:
Private

Academic Calendar:
Semester

Religious Affiliation:
Catholic (Jesuit)

Founded:
1863

Web Site:
www.bc.edu

Main Phone:
(617) 552-8000

Admissions Phone:
(617) 552-3100

Student Body

**Full-Time
Undergraduates:**
9,059

**Part-Time
Undergraduates:**
0

**Total Male
Undergraduates:**
4,260

**Total Female
Undergraduates:**
4,799

Admissions

Overall Acceptance Rate:
32%

**Early Action
Acceptance Rate:**
43%

Regular Acceptance Rate:
29%

Total Applicants:
22,451

Total Acceptances:
7,178

Freshman Enrollment:
2,309

**Yield (% of admitted
students who actually enroll):**
32%

Early Decision Available?
No

Early Action Available?
Yes

Early Action Deadline:
November 11th

Early Action Notification:
December 25th

Regular Decision Deadline:
January 2nd

**Regular Decision
Notification:**
Before April 15th

Must-Reply-By Date:
May 1st

**Applicants Placed on
Waiting List:**
4,500

**Applicants Accepted From
Waiting List:**
2,000

**Students Enrolled From
Waiting List:**
165

**Transfer Applications
Received:**
942

**Transfer Applications
Accepted:**
240

Transfer Students Enrolled:
122

**Transfer Application
Acceptance Rate:**
25%

**Common Application
Accepted?**
Yes

Supplemental Forms?
Boston College Supplemental
Application

Admissions E-Mail:
ugadmis@bc.edu

Admissions Web Site:
*www.bc.edu/admission/
undergrad*

SAT I or ACT Required?
Yes

→

**SAT I Range
(25th–75th Percentile):**
1240–1410

**SAT I Verbal Range
(25th–75th Percentile):**
610–700

**SAT I Math Range
(25th–75th Percentile):**
630–710

Retention Rate:
95%

**Top 10% of
High School Class:**
74%

Application Fee:
$60

SAT II Requirements:
For all applicants, the Writing
and Foreign Language tests are
recommended; for the Accelerated Medical and Accelerated
Dental Programs: Chemistry,
Mathematics Level II, and Writing are required, and a
foreign language test is
strongly recommended.

**SAT II Requirements
for the University
Professors:**
For all applicants, the
Literature, Foreign Language,
and Mathematics tests are
recommended.

Financial Information

Full-Time Tuition:
$31,438

Room and Board:
$10,845

Books and Supplies:
$650 per year

**Average Need-Based
Financial Aid Package
(including loans, work-study,
grants, and other sources):**
$27,292

**Students Who
Applied For Financial Aid:**
53%

Students Who Received Aid:
40%

Financial Aid Forms Deadline:
February 1

Financial Aid Phone:
(800) 294-0294

Financial Aid E-Mail:
student.services@bc.ed

Financial Aid Web Site:
www.bc.edu/offices/stserv/
financial

Academics

The Lowdown On...
Academics

Degrees Awarded:
Bachelor
Doctorate
First Professional
Master
Post Master

Most Popular Majors:
10% Finance
9% English
9% Communications
7% Economics
7% History

Undergraduate Schools:
Arts and Sciences
Carroll School of Management
Connell School of Nursing
Lynch School of Education
Rehabilitation Sciences
Sargent College of Health and
University Professors Program

→

Full-Time Faculty:
660

Average Course Load:
15 credits (5 courses)

Faculty with Terminal Degree:
97%

Graduation Rates:
Four-Year: 87%
Five-Year: 89%
Six-Year: 89%

Student-to-Faculty Ratio:
14:1

Special Degree Options

BA-MA Degree Option—In five years, students can receive both their bachelor's and master's degrees.

AP Test Score Requirements

Possible credit for scores of 4 or 5

IB Test Score Requirements

Possible credit for scores of 6 or 7

Academic Clubs

Accounting Academy, Information Technology Club, Another Choice on Campus, Bellarmine Pre-Law Council, Black Law Students Association, Gold Key National Honor Society, Intellectual Property and Technology Forum, Political Science Association, Students for Corporate Citizenship of America

Best Places to Study

O'Neil Library, Bapst Library, Addie's, dorm study lounges

Did You Know?

There are no fewer than **six factions of the student government** at BC: CSOM Government, CSON Senate, LSOE Senate, Student Alumni Council, Undergraduate Government of Boston College, and Woods College of Advancing Studies Student Senate.

The 120 Jesuits living on the Boston College campus make up **the largest Jesuit community in the world**. About half are actively involved in the University's faculty and administration; 22 are graduate students from 10 foreign countries.

Students Speak Out On...
Academics

{ **"The teachers, for the most part, were fairly willing to accommodate students' needs. Most teachers take their jobs very seriously, and they're dedicated to challenging the students in their classes."**

Q "The classes are really good and I've had incredible professors so far. **It's not hard to get the classes you want**, but if they are closed then you can always get an override into the class or change it during the first week of the semester. It's known as drop/add."

Q "I am a biology major, and my introductory classes in the first year or two were rather large. **You'll have to go out of your way to get to know the professors**. They're always willing to help you, though, and as you focus in on your major, the classes become much smaller and you definitely get to know some professors very well. I've even had dinner at two of my professors' houses."

Q "I have had a bunch of **bad teachers in the computer science department**, but the teachers here are usually pretty varied."

Q "A **few teachers know how to teach**, but most are there for a paycheck, to hear themselves talk, or to fill quotas. Out of 38 classes at Boston College, I probably found a dozen or so interesting."

Q "The **professors here are absolutely wonderful**! Most of mine have reached out and really tried to get to know me as a person. Sometimes it is a good idea to attend their mandatory office hours so that they get to know you one-on-one, especially near grading time! However, most of the professors genuinely want to get to know their students, and many give out their home phone numbers in case we ever have burning questions."

Q "I've met some of the most amazing professors this year, but also some crappy ones. The best way to get good professors is to **go to www.ugbc.org and click on PEPs**, which are student evaluations of professors. It really helps for course selections."

Q "The **teachers are very knowledgeable** and most are very willing to give you any extra help you may need in their classes."

Q "As with any school, some teachers are terrific, others are not. No teacher, however, inspired me to pursue a career in their respective subject, which may or may not be a personal problem. **I think BC's arts and sciences core is rather extensive and tedious**. I still haven't applied "Chemistry and Society" or "Geo-science and Public Policy" to anything practical. After finishing the core requirements, I was able to pursue my greater interests. Accordingly, I found myself enjoying classes more in the latter part of my college education."

Q "Teachers are usually cool. I've **had some really good ones and a couple of really bad ones**. You'll find that almost anywhere, but I think that teachers here are ultimately looking after you to do well."

Q "I am an economics major and I love all of my economics professors. The **BC student government, the UGBC, updates the PEPs frequently on their Web site**. Try to check out the reviews about professors before you select a course! They are unbelievably helpful."

The College Prowler Take On...
Academics

It's fair to say that most, if not all, Boston College professors are extremely capable, and more often than not, they're ridiculously intelligent. However, competency and good nature don't necessarily always go hand in hand. Some of the professors are here just because it's their job, and some care but just don't know how to teach or help confused students understand better. Luckily, bad or misdirected professors are in the minority. Most of the professors at BC are passionate and extremely intelligent individuals who inspire their students to follow the BC motto, "Ever to excel."

Of course, there are a few bad apples that just can't seem to relate to their students, typically because of an age gap that can span decades. Unfortunately, many of these professors are tenured so there's little to no chance that they are leaving BC anytime soon. If the professor makes you queasy on the first day, then drop the class and add something else as soon as possible. To increase your chances of finding a good professor or interesting class, go to *ugbc.org* and check out the professor evaluations (PEPs), where previous students have chimed in with their two cents regarding the teacher's aptitude. The PEPs are usually right on target describing the positive and negative attributes of the teacher. There are plenty of great professors at BC, and there's no reason you should have to remain in a class where you feel hesitant to shine.

The College Prowler® Grade on
Academics: A-

A high Academics grade generally indicates that professors are knowledgeable, accessible, and genuinely interested in their students' welfare. Other determining factors include class size, how well professors communicate, and whether or not classes are engaging.

Local Atmosphere

The Lowdown On...
Local Atmosphere

Region:
New England

City, State:
Chestnut Hill, Massachusetts

Setting:
Suburban

Distance from NYC:
3.5 hours

Points of Interest:
Fenway Park
Freedom Trail
Boston Public Gardens

→

Closest Movie Theaters:

Circle Cinemas
399 Chestnut Hill Avenue
Brookline, MA 02135
(617) 566-4040

Closest Shopping Malls:

The Atrium
The Mall at Chestnut Hill

Major Sports Teams:

Boston Bruins (hockey)
Boston Celtics (basketball)
Boston Patriots (football)
Boston Red Sox (baseball)

City Web Sites

www.boston.com
www.boston-online.com

Did You Know?

5 Fun Facts about Boston:

- Boston boasts the nation's **first subway**, built in 1897.

- The John Hancock Building, Boston's tallest, was designed by **IM0 Pei**, who also designed the glass entrance at the Louvre.

- The Big Dig is the **most expensive highway project** in U.S. history, costing more than a billion dollars per mile.

- The Boston Red Sox played in the very first **World Series** in 1903 and won.

- Boston boasts **a quarter of a million students**, attending 50 colleges or universities in a fifty square mile area.

Famous Bostonians:

Aerosmith

Henry Adams

Samuel Adams

Ralph Waldo Emerson

Benjamin Franklin

Jack Lemmon

Samuel Morse

Leonard Nimoy

Edgar Allen Poe

Paul Revere

Mark Wahlberg

Barbara Walters

Local Slang:

Pahk your cah in the baack yaad – "Park your car in the backyard"

American chop suey - Macaroni with hamburger, tomato sauce, some onion, and green pepper

B'daydas – "Potatoes"

Barrel – Trash can

Bubbla – A water fountain

Elastics – Rubber bands

Frankfurt – Hot dog

Fried – Weird, bizarre

Onna-conna – "On account of"

Potty plattah – "Party platter"

Soap – Dirty hippy

Students Speak Out On...
Local Atmosphere

"Every year from September through May, Boston plays home to thousands of 18- to 22-year-olds. There are many, many schools in Boston. There are theatres, museums and historic sites. It has everything and anything."

Q "Boston is a college town, and anywhere you go you will see people your age. **There are literally some 50 colleges within a 15-mile radius**. Though we are technically in Chestnut Hill, we are only a half-hour train ride from Boston. There are many historic sites in close proximity, like Fenway Park, the Boston Public Gardens, Quincy Market and Faneuil Hall."

Q "Not only is Boston an incredible city with plenty of fun things to do, but it's also **the biggest college town in America**, meaning that there are tons of other universities and colleges that you can visit if there's nothing going on at BC."

Q "During the school months, a third of the people in Boston are under 25. Definitely do all the tourist stuff, like **going to Newbury Street and the Copley Mall to shop**, going to the North End for amazing Italian food, and going to a bar in Cambridge so that you can tell all your friends at home that you went to a Harvard bar and messed with the smart kids."

Q "Boston is a college town, and the city itself should definitely be taken advantage of because it is very easy to let yourself become isolated and never leave the campus. **I recommend visiting Faneuil Hall, the North End, the Wharves, Copley, and Newbury Street**."

Q "BC's partial isolation from downtown Boston is a wonderful thing. I was truly able to enjoy campus life, while also benefiting from the advantages of the city. It's a perfect balance. **There are tons of other universities and plenty of ways to satisfy your alternative interests in the city**. Go to Boston as frequently as possible and avoid the kids on campus with visors, bleached tips, and Abercrombie sportswear."

Q "You can't be bored here, ever. **Stay away from Roxbury; it's a bad neighborhood**, but you'll probably never be there anyway. The Saint Patrick's Day parade in Southie is a fun time. I recommend trying to visit Cape Cod when it gets warm."

Q "BC is surrounded by fantastic places to eat and hang out, which are all right on the T line. The T goes directly into Boston. I never lived here before, but **I can't imagine living anywhere else for college**. I live about five blocks from Boston College and have never been in a cooler place. Boston is full of great schools, including BU and Harvard, where the best men to date are, so the city atmosphere here caters to us students."

Q "I think BC is ideal because it's not exactly in the heart of the city. It's actually in a neighboring town, but **the city is only a T ride away**. This way you get the real college campus experience, since your campus isn't in the middle of a busy city, but you're close enough to the city that you don't feel like you're in the middle of nowhere. Sometimes you fall into a trap where you never make the effort to go into the city, which happened to me this year, but that's more of a personal choice."

Q "The atmosphere in Chestnut Hill is chill. It's 10 minutes from the city, but the town is beautiful and everywhere you go, whether it's across the street to Maddies, or to Newton Center, you're bound to run into classmates. We're close to BU, Northeastern, Harvard, Babson, Bentley and a bunch of other smaller schools. There are plenty of attractions, namely **the Museum of Fine Arts, the aquarium, the Charles River, the Fleet Center, and Fenway**. The only thing I'd stay away from would be the cops."

Q "I think that our campus is perfectly situated in a suburban town right next to the amazing city of Boston. The T, Boston's version of the subway, is located right at the foot of campus and it is even called the 'Boston College Line.' It only takes a few minutes to get into the city, where **dozens of other colleges and universities** are located: Boston University, Northeastern, Harvard, the Massachusetts Institute of Technology, etc."

The College Prowler Take On...
Local Atmosphere

Boston is a wonderful city with loads of American history on pretty much every corner. It is also chock-full of college-aged people, so the area definitely has that youthful, alive feel that a lot of places do not. Boston is fairly clean and efficient, and absolutely bursting with character. Massachusetts is one of those states that actually feels significantly culturally distinct from other states. When you're there, you're very aware of talking to Bostonians, eating Boston food and soaking up what is a distinctly "Boston vibe."

Boston College is located right on the outskirts of the Boston metropolis, which gives BC students a mix of low-key suburbia and thrilling city living. Harvard, Northeastern, and Tufts are all fairly close to BC, as are many other colleges. However, that doesn't mean you'll ever actually see or talk to a student at one of these universities, as some BC students tend to find friends only on Chestnut Hill. Other people are out there, beyond the gates of Chestnut Hill, but you have to be open to finding them. Try to remember that there are other kinds of people nearby, in case you ever want to expand your horizons or see what life is like beyond the college. Definitely visit Faneuil Hall, the Boston Common, Harvard Square, and the Freedom Trail. One of the worst mistakes you can make is to stay on Chestnut Hill and put off exploring the awesome city that surrounds you. There is so much character to Boston, but you have to be willing to venture out and experience something more than just the few blocks that circle Boston College.

A

The College Prowler® Grade on
Local
Atmosphere: A

A high Local Atmosphere grade indicates that the area surrounding campus is safe and scenic. Other factors include nearby attractions, proximity to other schools, and the town's attitude toward students.

Safety & Security

The Lowdown On...
Safety & Security

Number of BC Police:
43 full-time police

BC Police Phone:
(617) 552-4444 (emergencies)
(617) 552-4440

Safety Services:
Eagle Escort
Eagle Eye on Crime
Emergency Blue-Lights
RAD Training
Victim's Resource Manual

Health Services:
Allergy clinic
Immunizations
Nutrition clinic
Routine physical examinations
Skin clinic
Some on-site pharmaceuticals
Physical therapy
Women's health clinic

Health Center Office Hours:
Monday–Friday,
8 a.m.–5 p.m.

Did You Know?

The Boston College Police Department (BCPD) officers are **granted police authority** while on campus by the Commonwealth of Massachusetts, as well as deputy sheriff powers for when they're in off-campus situations.

Students Speak Out On...
Safety & Security

"Security and safety are outstanding. I had a summer class that ended at 8 p.m. and I parked off-campus. I never even gave it a second thought."

Q "I have **never felt unsafe around Boston College**. You just have to be smart and use common sense whenever you leave campus."

Q "Chestnut Hill is a quaint town, so **there's not much to worry about** walking through campus at night. Certain areas around campus are sometimes dangerous late at night, but actual on-campus safety is really good at BC."

Q "**Our campus is extremely safe**. It is located in one of the wealthiest suburban areas around, and we're not directly in the city. We have our own police force and escorts who will travel with you if you ever think you might need them. I have never felt scared walking alone at night since there are always people around."

Q "You just have to make sure you take the proper precautions while walking around, but it's all very well lit and **there are emergency lights with phones that connect directly to the BCPD everywhere**."

Q "**Women are not allowed to live on the first floor of any dorm freshman year**, which can ease a lot of concerns about female safety."

Q "The campus is not overwhelmingly large, but it can be somewhat frightening for a freshman walking alone at night. As a result, **BC has an extremely reliable escort service that will take a student to and from any destination on campus** or in close proximity. Also, there are bright blue-light call stations everywhere that a student can utilize at any time to immediately contact the police. Word to the wise: never hit the blue button unless you are in a real emergency!"

Q "Boston College is ridiculously safe. The **Boston College police force is notorious for being everywhere**, much to students' annoyance and parents' relief. The very first week of school, freshmen are required to attend a safety-information assembly, one that gives such disturbing national statistics that departing seniors still recall the frightening facts presented at the meeting. As a result, students are keenly aware of the dangers that are possible, yet with the BCPD around, they know that they're highly unlikely to ever occur."

Q "I feel that campus is pretty safe. The Boston College Police Department is always patrolling and making sure things are going well. There are also **blue-lights and emergency call-boxes located all around campus**. The BCPD has a very quick response time and the officers are very polite. Also, the dorms use key cards, which only allow access into certain dorms. For instance, one person's ID works only for the Newton Campus dorms, and another person's ID works only for the College Road dorms, so strangers can't get into the dorms very easily."

Q "Try to **get a job on the BC escort service, since you get paid pretty much to sit around**. It's rare that a student actually feels nervous about walking home from the library."

Q "**Security is actually amazing**. I know from personal experience. It's a very long story, but I was threatened earlier this semester and the BCPD were so great to me."

Q "On campus, **I never feel unsafe walking alone at any time of night**. There are areas around campus, like Reservoir, Cleveland Circle, and Commonwealth Avenue, that can be a little scary. I bet there is probably only one assault case per year in these places at night. My friends and I just have a 'never go home alone' policy in order to avoid any problems."

Q "It's a pretty safe campus, with blue-lights and call-boxes located all around so that you can call the BC police in case of an emergency. There is a **BC escort service that you can use if you want a ride back to your dorm**, to campus from your dorm or to local areas near BC. There are also BC escort people who can walk you to and from your dorm or the library."

Q "The BCPD is the campus security force and **they help you out with whatever you need** in terms of your safety. If you are worried about being safe at BC, you don't have to be, even though it is in Boston."

Q "Our campus is pretty safe and secure. **We have an on-campus police force that drives around late at night**, and there are 'safe stations' too, which have buttons that you push in case of an emergency and they instantly inform the police about where you are, and then lights start flashing, etc. They are usually located at bus stations or just randomly around campus."

Q "The BCPD moved to a new building on lower campus, and is now right next to Hillside and the smaller bookstore. All traffic violations are taken care of there as well. The new location for the BCPD makes them more apparent on campus, since **they are located on a major walking route**."

The College Prowler Take On...
Safety & Security

All in all, Boston College is a safe place for students to go to school and hang out. During the first week of school, mandatory meetings give students the emergency and non-emergency information on locating and contacting the police. Incoming students are made aware of the potential dangers around them and are told about the best ways to avoid being victimized in any way. Also, police officers are always extremely friendly and helpful. Since it is such a safe environment, no one is ever too busy to tend to whatever small concern you might have. If something were to go wrong, they would come to your rescue immediately and do everything they could to help you.

Chestnut Hill is so safe that it's almost embarrassing. Not that nothing bad ever happens here, but it is extremely rare. In all likelihood, you'll never need to use the call boxes scattered around campus, but their presence radiates a constant feeling of security around the college grounds. The escort service is a wonderful addition to the safety on campus. Most students find it very reassuring that they can pick up a phone and have the school come pick them up. The BCPD always looks for ways to contribute to the students' feeling of well-being. When you leave campus, though, you should probably be a little more careful. Boston is a pretty safe city, but you do need to be a little more cautious.

A+

The College Prowler® Grade on

Safety & Security: A+

A high grade in Safety & Security means that students generally feel safe, campus police are visible, blue-light phones and escort services are readily available, and safety precautions are not overly necessary.

Computers

The Lowdown On...
Computers

High-Speed Network?
Yes

Number of Labs:
1

Wireless Network?
Yes

Operating Systems:
Windows XP Professional,
Mac OS X

Free Software

Adobe Acrobat Reader, Apple QuickTime Player, McAfee Virex for Macintosh, McAfee VirusScan for Windows, Microsoft Internet Explorer, Microsoft Outlook Express, Netscape Mail, Netscape Navigator, Nortel Contivity VPN Client, Oracle CorporateSync Palm, Campus Time, Oracle CorporateTime, RealOne Player, Tera Term Pro for Windows, TN3270, WinImage, WinZip

Discounted Software

Mathematica, Adobe Acrobat, HyperRESEARCH, SAS, SPSS, RATS, Matlab, Scientific WorkPlace

24-Hour Labs

No

Charge to Print?

No

Did You Know?

If you go to the lab and forget to bring your floppy to save your work, you're not out of luck. There are **floppy disc vending machines** for your convenience.

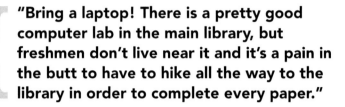

Students Speak Out On...
Computers

"Bring a laptop! There is a pretty good computer lab in the main library, but freshmen don't live near it and it's a pain in the butt to have to hike all the way to the library in order to complete every paper."

Q "I would suggest bringing your own computer if you have one. **Each person gets their own internet hook-up** and phone line in the dorms. But if you don't bring one, there is a perfectly good computer lab that generally isn't very crowded. So, it's up to you."

Q "The network is kind of slow compared to other places, but it is still significantly better than a modem. It is comparable to the cable modem that I have at home. I don't really visit the computer lab too often, except to print stuff, but it seems that it doesn't get too crowded. **I would suggest your own computer** if you can bring one. You basically need it as a word processor and for recreational Internet activity."

Q "I would recommend bringing your own computer, although one could survive without. **The computer labs are often crowded**, particularly when you need one most. I don't spend much time on the computer, but I never had much trouble with the network. It is prone to temporary shutdowns, but nothing of grave concern."

Q "I check my e-mail frequently, and it's nice that **BC has random public computers set up around campus**, like in Starbucks and outside the Rat, so I can easily check my e-mail from outside of my dorm."

Q "There is an **optional BC computer package that students can purchase** before arriving on campus freshman year. This option takes away the stress of finding your own laptop and printer during the hectic weeks before school starts. You can pick up the package on campus as soon as you arrive on campus and are settled in."

Q "**Having your own computer is nearly essential** at BC. The Ethernet provides a super fast connection to the Internet, the network neighborhood, and anything that you would need to be online for. All of this is available in the school computer labs, but they aren't open 24 hours a day and you won't have the freedom that you will with your own laptop or PC."

Q "The network is good. I don't usually have many problems with it going down and it's usually really fast. **The labs are crowded during peak hours like right before a common class time**, usually with people printing things out. IBM's usually go first, but if you like Macs then there is never any wait. I have my own laptop and it's the best thing in the world, in my opinion. I usually take it to work or to the lab and then I never have to wait for a computer. Everyone I know has their own computer, but it's not necessary."

Q "Our computer lab is a great resource, but most students bring their own computers. BC sends out information about buying a computer over the summer before freshman year. If you buy that computer through BC, they will fix it for no charge if there's ever a problem. However, it's not necessary that you have your own computer since the computer lab is always available. **It's simply more convenient to have your own**."

Q "The computer labs are pretty good. I use them a lot just because I get too easily distracted in my own room around my friends. The labs are not usually crowded, unless it's finals time. But, **I would bring your own computer just for the convenience**, even though it's not necessary."

Q "You have the same e-mail address and voicemail number for four and a half years. You keep it for six months after you graduate, which is really awesome, and you can even check your voicemail over the Internet. I think it's even easier than doing it over the phone. However, you should get your own computer. The **school provides computers for pretty cheap prices**, should you choose to buy from them. I'd suggest a laptop for portability, like when you want to take it to the library to get away from your room to study."

Q "BC typically has used *ontheroad.bc.edu* as the home address for e-mail, however a new site is up and running for students to utilize. ***Webmail.bc.edu* is a much more current and innovative site for e-mail use**."

The College Prowler Take On...
Computers

Boston College maintains an efficient and up-to-date computer lab that is only marginally crowded during exams. Even when the labs are crowded or you have some kind of computer problem, the lab employees are generally very helpful. Despite the general accessibility of the labs, most students have their own computers. Since most of the people at BC frequently check their e-mail and use Instant Messenger, the convenience of having a personal computer in your own room can't be beat. Certain majors, such as English or history, require much more writing than other areas where an individual computer might not be mandatory. It really all depends on the classes you are taking and what you want to use your computer for.

The school also helps out students who do wish to own a computer by offering the option to buy a computer through the university. Doing this gives you the chance to have your computer fixed free of charge. The network may not be the fastest in the world, but the freedom offered by wireless connections is certainly a plus. The lab is a noteworthy resource, but most students agree that having a computer of your own is preferable to relying on the Campus Technology Resource Center.

B+

The College Prowler® Grade on

Computers: B+

A high grade in Computers designates that computer labs are available, the computer network is easily accessible, and the campus' computing technology is up-to-date.

Facilities

The Lowdown On...
Facilities

Athletic Center:
Conte Forum

Libraries:
2, Bapst Library and O'Neill
Library

Student Center:
No specific building; McElroy
Commons is the closest thing

Campus Size:
240 acres

Popular Places to Chill:
Hillside
The Quad

What Is There to Do on Campus?

Well, you should be learning, but there's always people-watching in the Quad, or in front of Lower. You can play sports or go hot-tubbing in the Plex. Perhaps you might want to have snowball fights or go sledding around campus during the winter months. There are many sporting events to attend throughout the year as well!

Students love to go to sporting events, which generally include going to parties before or after the game, or maybe both. There is no real student union for students to hang out in, but they make up for it by creating their own fun. Go into Boston for a movie or to go shopping. Go ice-skating, sledding or bowling.

Movie Theater on Campus?

No

Bowling on Campus?

No

Bar on Campus?

No

Coffeehouse on Campus?

Yes, Starbucks

Students Speak Out On...
Facilities

"Many of the dorms have secret little work-out rooms in the basements. Fenwick, 90, Edmonds, Vanderslice, and Voute all have weight rooms that never get crowded."

Q "The athletic facility on campus, which is called the **Plex, is pretty nice**. The roof of the Plex is an eyesore, but on the plus side, it has an indoor track, pool, weights, cardio equipment, basketball, tennis, racquetball and squash courts, and aerobic classes like step and yoga, all of which are free. There's no official student center as of yet, another campus joke, but McElroy is kind of like BC's version of a student center."

Q "The BC facilities are, for the most part, fine. The **dormitories are actually quite nice**. The Plex, which is the gym, is kind of small given the size of the school's population. It is always overcrowded and insanely hot in the late afternoons. A lot of people work out outside as well."

Q "**We don't have a student center**, but I hear they're constructing one which, shockingly, coincides with my departure. The athletic facility has to be the worst recreational center in all of Division I colleges. It doesn't seem fair to pay $35,000 to share a weight machine with 9,000 other students."

Q "**We have a pretty big gym on the main campus called the Plex**. Since I live on Newton campus, I never go there. I just go to the one on Newton campus, which is kind of small, but is okay for what I need to do. It has a treadmill, bikes, StairMasters and a weight room with about 10 different machines. It's much smaller than the Plex, but it is fine for me. Plus, it never gets really crowded."

Q "**The Plex could be better**. You have to sign up for machines early in the morning if you want to get one for later in the day. Yet it is a vast improvement from what it used to be!"

Q "Some facilities are state-of-the-art, while others need some work. For example, the football, basketball, and hockey facilities (Alumni Stadium and Conte Forum) are great, but **the recreation complex is terrible**. The computer center is nice, and fairly efficient. We have the worst student center I have seen in all the colleges I have visited!"

Q "**Upper campus had a major remodeling job**, so many of the dorms are updated and connected, which adds to a sense of community for the freshmen. These new conglomerations of buildings have really nice study rooms with vending machines and some have laundry rooms in the basement."

Q "Facilities are great. The gym is a little lame, which is surprising for a Division I school, but it gets the job done. It has a nice track and tennis courts and lots of cardio equipment. **There are great libraries and other student buildings and a big computer lab**."

Q "The sports complex was redone. **It is really nice and offers weights, machines, and classes** such as yoga. The pools and courts are also available for student use. The library, computer center, and the Academic Development Center are also very nice."

Q "The facilities are pretty nice. **Most of the stuff is fairly new**, but the one thing that I am disappointed in is the athletic complex for non-athletes. The computer center is really nice and we have several libraries at our disposal."

Q "**Two buildings were constructed on campus**. One is Merkert, where most science classes are taken. That building is ridiculously nice, but usually only bio and other types of science majors get the chance to utilize the structure. The other building is commonly referred to as Hillside, because of the fantastic new dining hall in the base of the building. This building also has tons of teacher offices, a smaller bookstore, the BCPD office, and can be accessed from either the street or from the elevator out of O'Neill library."

Q "The lack of a strong student center can make the campus seem much bigger than it is. After leaving high school, where the cafeteria or senior lounge gave students a place to all convene, it was strange to come to BC and realize that there was no singular place that everyone can come together. **The dustbowl and the Quad are alright**, but a student union might be a nice addition for the school to consider."

The College Prowler Take On...
Facilities

Throughout the last few years, the school has undergone a complete campus beautification program, and the results are awesome. Two buildings were added, as well as a new dining hall and new routes for walking through campus. The athletic center for the athletes is excellent, or so the non-athletes are told. As great as it is, only a small portion of campus is allowed to use it, and students gave mixed reviews of the ordinary fitness facility, the Plex. It's much better than it used to be, and it offers a lot to do, but it still can feel dark, dingy, and crowded.

Reviews were certainly not mixed about the student center. McElroy, which currently acts as a student union, should never be called a student union. It has two chairs, a couch and a few vending machines. This may change in the near future, as a new building is being planned and constructed, but in the meantime, McElroy leaves a lot to be desired. The campus itself, on the other hand, is beautiful. Its gothic architecture and its newer buildings are certainly praiseworthy. With the exception of the virtually non-existent student union and the small, ugly athletic facility for non-athletes, the facilities on campus are great.

B+

The College Prowler® Grade on

Facilities: B+

A high Facilities grade indicates that the campus is aesthetically pleasing and well-maintained; facilities are state-of-the-art, and libraries are exceptional. Other determining factors include the quality of both athletic and student centers and an abundance of things to do on campus.

Campus Dining

The Lowdown On...
Campus Dining

Freshman Meal Plan Requirement?

Yes

Meal Plan Average Cost:

$1,825 (flat rate without buying any extra Eagle Bucks)

Places to Grab a Bite with Your Meal Plan:

The Balcony

Food: Soups, salads, sandwiches, desserts

Location: Corcoran Commons

(The Balcony, continued)

Hours: Sunday–Thursday 3:30 p.m.–9:30 p.m.

The Bean Counter

Food: Coffee, tea, cleverly-named pre-made sandwiches

Location: Fulton Hall

Hours: Monday–Thursday 4 p.m.–8 p.m.

Beans, Creams, Dreams

Food: Ice cream, hot dogs

Location: Lower Campus Dining Facility

Hours: Seasonal

Carney's
Food: Breakfast

Location: McElroy Commons

Hours: Monday–Thursday
7:30 a.m.–12 a.m., Friday
7:30 a.m.–2 a.m., Saturday
8 a.m.–2 a.m.,
Sunday 8 a.m.–12 a.m.

The Chocolate Bar
Food: Coffee, desserts

Location: McElroy Commons

Hours: Monday–Thursday
8 a.m.–10 p.m., Friday 8 a.m.–
12 a.m., Saturday 12 p.m.–
12 a.m., Sunday 12 p.m.–
8 p.m.

Eagle's Nest
Food: Sandwiches, entrees

Location: McElroy Commons

Hours: Monday–Thursday
11 a.m.–4:30 p.m., Friday
11 a.m.–3 p.m.

Hillside Café
Food: Paninis, salads, deli

Location: Lower Campus
Administrative Building

Hours: Monday–Thursday
7:30 a.m.–8 p.m., Friday
7:30 a.m.–4 p.m., Saturday
(only during a home football
game) 3:30 p.m.–7:30 p.m.

Lower Live
Food: Taqueria, grill,
international entrees, soups

Location: Corcoran Commons

(Lower Live, continued)
Hours: Monday–Wednesday
6:30 a.m.–12 a.m., Thursday–
Friday 6:30 a.m.–2 a.m.,
Saturday 7:30 a.m.–2 a.m.,
Sunday 7:30 a.m.–12 a.m.

Lyons Hall (The Rat)
Food: Soups, sandwiches

Location: Lyons Hall

Hours: Monday–Friday
7:30 a.m.–3:30 a.m.

Off-Campus Places to Use Your Meal Plan:
Angora Too Café, Boloco,
Eagle's Deli, Flatbreads Café,
Mr. G's College Sub Shop,
Roggie's, The Avenue Grill,
Uno Chicago Grill

24-Hour On-Campus Eating?
No, but late night begins at
9 p.m. on lower campus.

Other Options
You could always have Pizzeria
Uno or Domino's deliver
a pizza to your room, and
you could still pay with your
meal plan. It's like going off
campus without having to go
anywhere.

Student Favorites
Make-your-own Belgian waffles
at Lower; Muffins at McElroy;
the New England Classic
at Hillside.

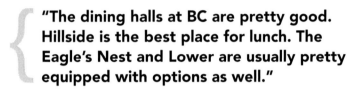

Students Speak Out On...
Campus Dining

{ **"The dining halls at BC are pretty good. Hillside is the best place for lunch. The Eagle's Nest and Lower are usually pretty equipped with options as well."**

Q "The only food on campus is the dining halls, unless you get a Chi Chi sausage after the bar on Thursday, Friday, or Saturday nights. But other than that, if you want to eat on campus, it's going to be in a dining hall. **The dining halls aren't bad, but they're not usually great**. There are a million places all around campus where you can order food for delivery. You can always find something you like to eat in Boston."

Q "Although I don't really have a basis for comparison, I understand that the food on campus is great. The exorbitant price aside, the **food has never posed a problem for me**. I really enjoyed the posh and cozy Hillside Café, complete with made-to-order sandwiches and Starbucks."

Q "**The food is actually really good**, although any campus food gets a little monotonous. Go visit your friends at other schools and you will appreciate BC food so much more."

Q "The food isn't bad for dining hall food. **Lunch at the Eagle's Nest deli is my favorite**, and there are a lot of good take out/delivery places around like Pic-A-Pasta and New Hong Kong."

Q "**There are three dining halls on the main Chestnut Hill campus** and one on Newton campus. The three on the main campus are there just to accommodate the size of the campus. One of them has a sandwich and wrap place, one has fast food, and the other has all of the above but to a lesser extent."

Q "I live on Newton campus, and the **food is okay at Stuart dining hall** at first, but there's not much of a selection and you get sick of it after a while. I think that's the case at every school, though. If you live on the upper campus, the food is better and there's more of a selection at the McElroy dining hall."

Q "**On-campus food is surprisingly good**. Sometimes there are even theme nights with guest chefs!"

Q "There are basically three major dining halls and three smaller ones. McElroy is where freshmen primarily eat, or at Stuart on Newton Campus, and Lower is where upperclassmen eat, both of which have just about everything. Chicken, pasta, salads and sandwiches are pretty much the standard at both places. Breakfasts are awesome at BC, but the omelet line can be super long. For lunch, a lot of people like the Rat for fast food type meals and the Eagle's Nest for sandwiches, salads, or soup. Hillside is a new and very popular addition to BC, and **they have awesome sandwiches** and a Starbucks as well. Watch out for the lines!"

Q "The food is pretty good. When I have friends visit from other schools, they always comment on how good it is. The pizza is their personal favorite. **One of the most frequented places for lunch is the Rat**, which may sound disgusting but it has really good lunch food like chicken fingers, burgers, fries, etc."

Q "The food isn't bad. There are a few dining halls, like McElroy, which is located on upper-middle campus and serves all kinds of food. A lot of freshmen that live on upper campus go there to eat. There is also the Eagle's Nest right below **McElroy, which serves wraps and salads but can get insanely crowded**. The Rat is located in the Quad, in the Lyons building, and is like McDonald's—serving fast and fried food. I usually go there to eat. Lower Dining Hall is on lower campus, where upperclassmen mostly go because it is closer to where they live. But anyone can go there, and I do see some underclassmen there, too. There is also Addie's, which is located above Lower and serves pretty much just pasta."

Q "The meal card is such a huge convenience at BC, because you never realize how expensive some of the food is that you're eating because it just gets deducted from your meal points. However, now that **our meal cards can be used at Flatbreads, and Pizzeria Uno on Harvard Avenue**, you might never need to eat at a dining hall again."

The College Prowler Take On...
Campus Dining

The food at Boston College is excellent, but it can just feel monotonous after a while. Dietary concerns are very important to BC, and the school does its best to provide a nice variety of foods for students with special or specific dietary needs. The freshmen eat at either Stuart or McElroy, and most seem to prefer the former to the latter. The Rat is the fast food spot on campus, with the best French fries and chicken fingers in the free world, or at least as far as we're concerned. Any student can eat at any dining hall. Some are just closer to certain dorms than others, and therefore attract certain students.

The newer dining hall, Hillside, has overpriced gourmet sandwiches, but using your trusty meal card allows the price to be a distant memory. BC has also started allowing students to use their pre-paid meal cards at off-campus locations like Pizzeria Uno and Flatbreads. This is by far one of the greatest ideas the administration has conjured up for BC students in quite a while, since it adds so much more variety to the students' dining options. Whether it's on or off campus, you'll be able to find food that tickles your taste buds and can be paid for with your meal plan.

B

The College Prowler® Grade on
Campus Dining: B

Our grade on Campus Dining addresses the quality of both school-owned dining halls and independent on-campus restaurants as well as the price, availability, and variety of food.

Off-Campus Dining

The Lowdown On...
Off-Campus Dining

Restaurant Prowler:
Popular Places to Eat!

Angora Café

Food: American, coffee

1024 Commonwealth Avenue Brighton, MA

(617) 232-1757

Cool Features: The best frozen yogurt, wraps, roll-ups and gourmet coffee in Boston.

(Angora Café, continued)

Hours: Monday–Saturday 8 a.m.–12 a.m., Sunday 9 a.m.–12 a.m.

Anna's Taqueria

Food: Mexican

1412 Beacon Street

(617) 739-7300

Price: $6–$10

Cool Features: Good, affordable Mexican food

Hours: Daily 10 a.m.–11 p.m.

→

The Blue Ribbon BBQ

Food: BBQ

908 Massachusetts Avenue
Arlington, MA

(781) 648-7427

Cool Features: It's the best
BBQ in town.

Price: $10–$16

Hours: Monday–Saturday
11:30 a.m.–9 p.m., Sunday
12 p.m.–8 p.m.

The Border Café

Food: Mexican

32 Church Street
Cambridge, MA

(617) 864-6100

Cool Features: The best
and most reasonably priced
Mexican food ever!

Price: $6–$10

Hours: Monday–Thursday
11 a.m.–12:45 a.m., Friday–
Saturday 11 a.m.–1:45 a.m.,
Sunday 12 p.m.–12:45 a.m.

The Cactus Club

Food: Mexican/Southwest

939 Boyleston Street

(617) 236-0200

Price: $8–$12

Hours: Monday–Wednesday
4 p.m.–10 p.m., Thursday
11:30 a.m.–11 p.m., Friday
11:30 a.m.–12 a.m., Sunday
11:30 a.m.–10 p.m.

The Cheesecake Factory

Food: American

300 Boyleston Street

(617) 964-3001

Cool Features: The menu is
the size of a book!

Price: $12–$20

Hours: Monday–Friday
11:30 a.m.–11:30 p.m.,
Saturdays 11:30 a.m.–
12:30 a.m.

CitySide Bar & Grille

Food: American

1960 Beacon Street

(617) 566-1002

Price: $8–$12

Hours: Sunday–Wednesday
11:30 a.m.–10 p.m.,
Thursday–Saturday
11:30 a.m.–10:30 p.m.

Espresso Royale Caffe

Food: Coffee, pastries

736 Commonwealth Avenue

(617) 277-8737

www.espressoroyale.com

Price: $5–$7

Hours: Daily 8 a.m.–3 p.m.

Eagle's Deli

Food: American

1918 Beacon Street

(617) 731 3232

Cool Features: The most impossibly huge hamburgers in the history of human endeavors. One weighs over five pounds.

Price $7–$12

Hours: Daily 8 a.m.–11 p.m.

The Fireplace

Food: American

1634 Beacon Street

(617) 975-1900

Price: $15–$30

Hours: Monday–Wednesday 5:30 p.m.–12 a.m., Thursday–Sunday 11 a.m.–1 a.m.

Fire + Ice

Food: American/Vegetarian

205 Berkeley Street

(617) 338-4019

Cool Features: There is a long bar of raw vegetables and meats, and you get a bowl to fill with whatever you want and as much as the bowl can hold. You even get to pick your own seasoning sauce from about a dozen options. They have a gigantic grill in the middle of the

(Fire + Ice, continued)

dining room where they cook your creation, which you can put over rice or on a tortilla.

Price: $10–$22

Hours: Sunday–Thursday 11:30 a.m.–10 p.m., Friday–Saturday 11:30 a.m.–11 p.m.

Flatbreads Café

Food: Pizza, sandwiches

11 Commonwealth Avenue

(617) 964-8484

Price: $7–$10

Hours: Daily 8 a.m.–7 p.m.

Fresh City

Food: Wraps, sandwiches, stir-fry

201 Brookline Avenue

(617) 424-7907

Price: $8–$10

Hours: Monday–Friday 6:30 a.m.–5 p.m.

Fugakyu

Food: Japanese

280 Beacon Street

(617) 734-1268

www.fugakyujapanese.com

Price: $10–$22

Hours: Sunday–Saturday 11:30 a.m.–3 p.m., 5 p.m.–2 a.m.

Golden Temple

Food: Chinese

1651 Beacon Street

(617) 277-9722

Price: $8–$12

Hours: Monday–Thursday
11 a.m.–1 a.m.,
Friday–Sunday
11 a.m.–2 a.m.

Lucky Wah

Food: Chinese

1391 Beacon Street

(617) 566-1002

Price: $8–$14

Hours: Daily 12 p.m.–2 a.m.

Mr. G's College Sub Shop

Food: Sub sandwiches

2197 Commonwealth Avenue

(617) 787-1171

Price: $6–$10

Hours: Daily 9 a.m.–7 p.m.

Pino's Pizza

Food: Pizza

1920 Beacon Street

(617) 566-6468

Price: $5–$8

Hours: Monday–Friday
11 a.m. –1 a.m., Saturday–
Sunday 11 a.m.–12 a.m.

Roggie's

Food: American

356 Chestnut Hill Avenue

(617) 566-1880

Price: $8–$14

Hours: Daily 11 a.m.–2 a.m.

The Sunset Grille

Food: American

130 Brighton Avenue

(617) 254-1331

Cool Features: Awesome
burgers and many different
types of beer.

Hours: Monday–Saturday
11:30 a.m.– 1 a.m.,
Sunday 11 a.m.–1 a.m.

T-Anthony's

Food: Italian/Pizza

1016 Commonwealth Avenue

(617) 734-7708

Cool Features: BU
paraphernalia covers the
walls, and its always packed
with students.

Price: $2–$10

Hours: 7 a.m.–1 a.m.

Vinny T's of Boston

Food: Italian

1700 Beacon Street

(617) 277-3400

Cool Features: This Italian eatery has the largest portions!

Hours: Monday–Thursday 4 p.m.–10 p.m., Friday 4 p.m.–11 p.m., Saturday 12 p.m.–11 p.m.

Wing It

Food: Wings

1153 Commonwealth Avenue

(617) 566-1002

Price: $8–$12

Hours: Saturday–Sunday 12 p.m.–12 a.m., Monday–Friday 4 p.m.–12 a.m.

Student Favorites:

CitySide Bar & Grille, Eagle's Deli, Vinny T's of Boston

Closest Grocery Store:

Star Market
1717 Beacon Street
Brookline, MA
(617) 566-1802

24-Hour Eating:

Yes, especially in Boston, but generally only in chains that are known for being open all night.

Other Places to Check Out:

Bagel Rising, Bangkok Bistro, Big A Deli, Bluestone Bistro, Capital Grill, Domino's, Ginza, Hard Rock Café, Kaya, Paris Café, Presto, Tasca, Tequila Sunrise, Tomato's, Uno Chicago Grill, The Wrap

Best Pizza:

Pino's Pizza

Best Chinese:

Lucky Wah

Best Breakfast:

Eagle's Deli

Best Wings:

Wing It

Best Healthy:

Fresh City

Best Place to Take Your Parents:

The Cheesecake Factory

Students Speak Out On...
Off-Campus Dining

{

"Restaurants off-campus are just fine. Most are cheap and convenient. I would recommend Anna's or Pino's for something quick and cheap. Also, there is plenty of stellar dining in Boston and its suburbs."

Q "**I like Fugakyu for sushi** and Vinnie T's for big portions of Italian food."

Q "**The restaurants around BC are excellent**. CitySide, the Cheesecake Factory, Figs, Tasca, Fugakyu and Kaya are just a few options!"

Q "Boston is right up the road, so anything you could want to eat is available . . . The **popular places right off-campus are Roggie's and CitySide**."

Q "Off-campus there are many good places to eat, since you are in the city of Boston. There are **small sandwich shops like the Wrap**, Chinese places like Golden Temple, bar and grille joints like Sunset Grille and CitySide, and the infamous pizza and more joint, Roggie's."

Q "The good thing about Boston College is that you're in Boston (or at least close enough to be considered to be in the city) and there are thousands of places to eat at or order from! Roggie's is the best pizza. **Definitely go to Vinny T's for Italian food**, and if you can make it to the Cheesecake Factory, it is definitely worth your while (they don't serve just cheesecake, they have a huge menu of all sorts of foods, all excellent), though it's a little expensive. You can also get Domino's on your meal card if you sign up for dining bucks, so that's pretty nice."

Q "Boston has such great food—can you say Hard Rock Café? **A local favorite is also Vinny T's**, which serves amazing Italian food."

Q "Boston is a great city for food, but you'd better **have a hell of a lot of money because off-campus dining gets really expensive**. Most people eat in the dining halls."

Q "Off-campus has some **good places nearby like Roggie's and CitySide**. Those are right by BC and there are always lots of BC people there. But you have the whole city at your fingertips and there are so many great places to eat in Boston. The North End is kind of like a Little Italy. That's a fun place to go, and Capital Grill is amazing."

Q "Off-campus, you have Boston. It doesn't take long at all to get there and you don't need a car because you have the T. **You can have any kind of food you want**; it's incredible. "

Q "There are tons of restaurants and take out places near campus. I can't even begin to list them because there are so many, but **popular ones are Roggie's, Bluestone Bistro, Golden Temple for scorpion bowling,** Uno's, and The Cheesecake Factory."

Q "Boston and Newton have a lot of good places to eat. Roggie's is the popular BC hangout. There is also **CitySide in Cleveland Circle**. My friends and I also like Fresh City and Sweet Tomatoes in Newton (you need a car to get to either) and the Paris Café, a crepe place in Coolidge Corner."

Q "**Restaurants in Boston are awesome**! You can get coupon books near McElroy dining hall's lobby where you'll find tons of discounts on restaurants. You can also use it as a directory to find good spots. Some of the most popular restaurants with the students are Bangkok Bistro, Anna's Taqueria, the Cheesecake Factory, Ginza, and Vinny T's. There are really way too many to name. Definitely go all around Chestnut Hill, Allston and Brighton area, Newton, and Cleveland Circle."

Q "There are tons of restaurants around BC and basically **any place that delivers will deliver to you until 3 a.m.**, so that's pretty convenient."

Q "**You must hit up Bagel Rising on Commonwealth Avenue** at the intersection of Harvard Avenue! The people that work there are hilarious, and the Tequila Sunrise is the best breakfast sandwich in the area. The coffee is excellent as well. Watch out for lines around noon."

Q "Boston has everything! **Check out FiRE + iCE at either Harvard Square in Cambridge or at the downtown Boston location**. It's an experience! The Mexican food at the Border Café is phenomenal and reasonably priced. Also, the Big A deli in Brighton has the most incredible chicken Parmesan sandwich."

Q "There is a **long-lived debate over which pizza place in Cleveland Circle is better—Pino's or Presto**. I believe there is no comparison. Pino's is the winner hands down! The Wrap next door to Presto isn't bad either, especially their smoothies."

The College Prowler Take On...
Off-Campus Dining

You'll find more than your fair share of scrumptious eateries in Boston. Plant-eaters take note that vegan, vegetarian, and sushi restaurants aren't available at the students' beck and call as in California or New York. Fresh seafood, surprisingly flavorful Mexican, and incredible Italian food can be found within walking distance from campus. Commonwealth Avenue runs adjacent to campus and there you can find a couple of above-average eateries. Flatbreads serves amazing sandwiches for breakfast, lunch, and dinner. The wrap-maker there is a wizard at making sandwiches efficiently and effectively. On the other side of the T depot is Mr. G's College Sub Shop, which certainly isn't Subway, but isn't a bad alternative to eating in the dining hall either. Espresso Royale Caffe has great pastries and an enjoyable atmosphere.

Travel a few minutes on the T down to Cleveland Circle and you'll find several delicious off-campus dining establishments. Roggie's has an incredible atmosphere. CitySide Bar & Grille is the real gem of Cleveland Circle, with incredible salads, huge entrees, and a fantastic upstairs deck swarming with people, especially during the warmer months. Cleveland Circle is also home to Thai food, wraps, three competing pizza joints, and Eagle's Deli. Eagle's Deli is a favorite of Boston College students, many of whom stumble in on the weekends blurry-eyed, hung over, and in desperate need of complex carbohydrates. Eagle's Deli never disappoints and their Godzilla burger is exactly as it sounds: a monster. Check out the photos on the wall of all those who have attempted finishing the Godzilla. It's *Guinness Book* material!

The College Prowler® Grade on

Off-Campus Dining: A

A high Off-Campus Dining grade implies that off-campus restaurants are affordable, accessible, and worth visiting. Other factors include the variety of cuisine and the availability of alternative options (vegetarian, vegan, Kosher, etc.).

Campus Housing

The Lowdown On...
Campus Housing

Room Types:
Traditional residence halls (double, triple, or quad rooms), suite-style (4,6,7,8, or 9 people), apartment-style (2 per room, 4 or 6 per apartment)

Best Dorms:
Upper, 90, Vanderslice, Voute, Gabelli, Mods

Worst Dorms:
Edmonds, Newton, Walsh

Undergrads Living on Campus:
80%

Number of Dormitories:
31

University-Owned Apartments
0

➡

Dormitories:

Newton Campus:

Cushing
Floors: 4
Total Occupancy: 113
Bathrooms: Communal
Coed: Yes, by floor
Residents: Freshmen
Room Types: Singles, doubles
Special Features: Lounge, laundry in the basement

Duchesne (East & West)
Floors: 4
Total Occupancy: 320
Bathrooms: Communal
Coed: Yes, by floor
Residents: Freshmen
Room Types: Quads, triples, singles, doubles
Special Features: Laundry room, TV in lounge

Hardey
Floors: 3
Total Occupancy: 208
Bathrooms: Communal
Coed: Yes, by floor
Residents: Freshmen

(Hardey, continued)
Room Types: Singles, doubles, triples, quads
Special Features: Cardio room, weight room, laundry, lounge

Keyes
Floors: 5
Total Occupancy: 398
Bathrooms: Communal
Coed: Yes, by floor
Residents: Freshmen
Room Types: Singles, doubles, triples, quads
Special Features: Laundry, cardio room, library, trash room, lounge, Keyes Entertainment Center

Upper Campus:

Cheverus
Floors: 3
Total Occupancy: 348
Bathrooms: Communal
Coed: Yes
Residents: Freshmen
Room Types: Singles, triples, quads
Special Features: Laundry, lounge

Claver

Floors: 4

Total Occupancy: 104

Bathrooms: Communal

Coed: Yes

Residents: Freshmen

Room Types: Doubles, triples, quads

Special Features: Laundry, lounge

CLXF Connector

Floors: 4

Total Occupancy: 22

Bathrooms: Private

Coed: Yes

Room Types: Singles, doubles, triples

Special Features: Library, four study lounges, laundry

Fenwick

Floors: 4

Total Occupancy: 132

Bathrooms: Communal

Coed: Yes

Residents: Freshmen

Room Types: Singles, doubles, triples

Special Features: Lounges

Fitzpatrick Gonzaga Connector

Floors: 3

Total Occupancy: 12

(Fitzpatrick Gonzaga Connector, continued)

Bathrooms: Communal

Coed: Yes

Room Types: Singles, quads

Special Features: Laundry, three study lounges

Fitzpatrick

Floors: 4

Total Occupancy: 125

Bathrooms: Communal

Coed: Yes

Residents: Freshmen

Room Types: Singles, doubles, triples, quads

Special Features: Study lounges

Gonzaga

Floors: 4

Total Occupancy: 249

Bathrooms: Communal

Coed: Yes

Residents: Freshmen

Room Types: Singles, doubles, triples, quads

Special Features: Study lounges

Kostka

Floors: 3

Total Occupancy: 216

Bathrooms: Communal

Coed: Yes

(Kostka, continued)
Residents: Freshmen
Room Types: Doubles, triples
Special Features: Study lounges

Loyola
Floors: 4
Total Occupancy: 216
Bathrooms: Communal
Coed: Yes
Residents: Freshmen
Room Types: Doubles, triples
Special Features: Laundry

Medeiros
Floors: 4
Total Occupancy: 90
Bathrooms: Semi-private
Coed: Yes
Residents: Freshmen
Room Types: Suites
Special Features: Six semi-private lounges

Shaw
Floors: 2
Total Occupancy: 20
Bathrooms: Communal
Coed: Yes
Residents: Freshmen
Room Types: Doubles, triples, quads
Special Features: Study lounge, kitchen

Xavier
Floors: 4
Total Occupancy: 116
Bathrooms: Communal
Coed: Yes
Residents: Freshmen
Room Types: Doubles, triples, quads
Special Features: Study lounge

College Road:

Roncalli
Floors: 4
Total Occupancy: 172
Bathrooms: Communal
Coed: Yes
Residents: Sophomores, juniors, seniors
Room Types: Doubles, triples, quads

Welch
Floors: 5
Total Occupancy: 195
Bathrooms: Communal
Coed: Yes
Residents: Sophomores, juniors, seniors
Room Types: Doubles, triples, quads
Special Features: TV lounge, laundry, two regular lounges

Williams

Floors: 4

Total Occupancy: 184

Bathrooms: Communal

Coed: Yes

Residents: Sophomores, juniors, seniors

Room Types: Doubles, triples, quads

Lower Campus:

66 Commonwealth Avenue

Floors: 4

Total Occupancy: 250

Bathrooms: Communal

Coed: Yes

Residents: Sophomores, juniors, seniors

Room Types: Singles, doubles, triples

Special Features: Recreation room, chapel, two music rooms, laundry, lounges

90 St. Thomas More

Floors: 6

Total Occupancy: 470

Bathrooms: Private

Coed: Yes

Residents: Sophomores, juniors, seniors

Room Types: Doubles, six-persons

(90 St. Thomas More, continued)

Special Features: Two cardio rooms, laundry, trash rooms, music room, weight room, TV lounge, library, seminar room

110 St. Thomas More

Floors: 6

Total Occupancy: 300

Bathrooms: Private

Coed: Yes

Residents: Sophomores, juniors, seniors

Room Types: Six- and eight-person suites

Special Features: Lounges, recreation room, laundry

Edmond's

Floors: 9

Total Occupancy: 1090

Bathrooms: Private

Coed: Yes

Residents: Sophomores, juniors, seniors

Room Types: Doubles

Special Features: Weight room, laundry, study lounge, trash room

Greycliff

Floors: 3

Total Occupancy: 75

Bathrooms: Shared

Coed: Yes

(Greycliff, continued)

Residents: Sophomores, juniors, seniors

Room Types: Singles, doubles

Special Features: Lounges

Gabelli

Floors: 5

Total Occupancy: 200

Bathrooms: Private

Coed: Yes

Residents: Sophomores, juniors, seniors

Room Types: Four- and six-person apartments/suites

Special Features: Recreation room, laundry, weight room, TV and study lounges

Ignacio

Floors: 6

Total Occupancy: 350

Bathrooms: Private

Coed: Yes

Residents: Sophomores, juniors, seniors

Room Types: Four- and six-person apartments/suites

Special Features: Lounges, recreation room, laundry

Modulars

Floors: 1 (ranch-style apartments)

Total Occupancy: 350

Bathrooms: Private

(Modulars, continued)

Coed: Yes

Residents: Sophomores, juniors, seniors

Room Types: Four- and six-person apartments/suites

Special Features: Apartment-style setting

Rubenstein

Floors: 6

Total Occupancy: 300

Bathrooms: Private

Coed: Yes

Residents: Sophomores, juniors, seniors

Room Types: Four- and six-person apartments/suites

Special Features: Lounges, recreation room, laundry

Vanderslice

Floors: 6

Total Occupancy: 400

Bathrooms: Private

Coed: Yes

Residents: Sophomores, juniors, seniors

Room Types: Seven-, eight-, and nine-person suites

Special Features: Kitchen, cabaret room, game room, laundry rooms, study/TV lounges

Voute
Floors: 5
Total Occupancy: 200
Bathrooms: Private
Coed: Yes
Residents: Sophomores, juniors, seniors
Room Types: Four- and six-person townhouses/suites
Special Features: Lounges, recreation room, laundry

Walsh
Floors: 8
Total Occupancy: 350
Bathrooms: Private
Coed: Yes
Residents: Sophomores, juniors, seniors
Room Types: Four- and eight-person suites
Special Features: Lounges, weight room, laundry, study rooms

Housing Offered:
Singles: 7%
Doubles: 47%
Triples/Suites: 18%
Apartment-Style: 22%
Other: 6%

Bed Type
Twin extra-long

Cleaning Service?
Yes, public areas only

What You Get
Bed, desk, chair, cable hookup, telephone hookup, internet hookup, closet, window shade

Also Available
Special interest housing

Students Speak Out On...
Campus Housing

{ **"All dorms, despite what people might say, are much nicer than dorms at other schools. You don't get much choice for freshman year, though."**

Q "You don't get much of a choice as a freshman, and you are basically put where you're put. **There are two main areas where freshmen live**: Upper campus and Newton campus. You have to take a bus to get to Newton, which is a major pain, so I'm told, but both places are decent. Upper is definitely better, though. You could also ask for substance-free housing, which is on Upper and is all doubles. But, be advised: if you get caught drunk or high in there, you get kicked out of housing."

Q "**You don't really get a choice on where you live**, but I was a Newton kid and I absolutely loved it. At first you might think it sucks and that the buses are annoying, but I wouldn't have traded it for the world. Newton just becomes its own little community and everyone knows everyone else. At least it feels like they do. From what I can tell, the Upper campus kids aren't as close or friendly, though they all think they're a lot cooler than we are. It's kind of a rivalry thing freshman year, Newton versus Upper, but it's fun and basically either place you get, you will love it and think that where you live is better."

Q "Avoid Newton campus! As a freshman, you get somewhat of a choice between the Upper and Newton campuses. **Newton campus is a 10 minute bus ride away from the main campus** and is composed of isolated freshmen. I strongly recommend Upper campus. Other than that, I think that most of the dorms on Upper campus are the same."

Q "As a freshman, **I lived on Upper campus, which is the best place for first-years to live**. I lived in Walsh as a sophomore, which is huge, and nicer than it looks. We have a cute, eight-person suite, which is nice and perfectly fine for a year. Even though others brag about Vanderslice, Walsh is practically the same on the inside and has the same, if not better, setup. It's just not as close to the Lower Dining Hall, which is all of like a hundred so steps away."

Q "After freshman year, you move, hopefully, to lower campus. **Walsh, 90, and Vanderslice are the dorms for sophomore year,** with Walsh being the most ghetto but the most fun as well. Edmonds is for four people and Walsh has four person rooms, but is typically more for eight people. There is another singles dorm off campus called Greycliff. Ignacio and Rubenstein are for seniors and are for six people. They have kitchens. Voute and Gabelli are the nicest dorms and are for four people. They both have townhouses, which have two floors, but only the lucky people get those through the lottery. Those dorms have kitchens, too."

Q "**Dorms are decent at Boston College**, and they are getting better as there have been many renovations in the past few years. All dorms are coed. They are coed by floor freshman year and by room every year after that. There are communal bathrooms, and the girls' bathrooms are always locked. Upperclassmen live in suite-style housing, some with kitchens. All seniors have kitchens."

Q "The dorms are really nice in comparison with other schools I visited. **The freshman dorms were just renovated** so they're really nice now. The only problem is that BC always accepts too many people, so you may end up in a forced triple—three people in a double-sized room. I ended up in that situation and it wasn't the end of the world. It is cramped, but you do survive and they give you some money back for having to do it."

Q "I live in a crappy dorm this year, but it is being renovated, so there will only be one crappy dorm left. Chances that you will get it are slim. Half of the freshmen live on the main campus and the other half live on **Newton campus, which is like a few minutes bus ride from the main campus**. They have buses running all the time, though. You don't really get a choice on where you live, but I was a Newton kid and I absolutely loved it. At first you might think it sucks and that the buses are annoying, but I wouldn't have traded it for the world. Newton just becomes its own little community and everyone knows everyone. At least it feels like they do. From what I can tell, the Upper campus kids aren't as close or friendly, though they all think they're a lot cooler than we are . . . It's kind of a rivalry thing freshman year, Newton versus Upper, but it's fun. And basically either place you get, you will love it and think that where you live is better."

Q "As an incoming freshman you will either be placed on Upper campus, which is really nice and where I lived as a freshman, or on Newton campus, which is being done over so all of the dorms on **Newton will be brand new except Hardy/Cushing**. The only catch to living on Newton is that you have to take a bus to the main campus where your classes are. Here's a hint: if you are interested in specialty housing, like substance-free housing (which isn't really substance free) or the music floor, then you will automatically get a double on Upper."

Q "**Dorms are good, especially if you are lucky in the lotteries**. For freshman year it doesn't matter whether you pick Upper or Newton; everyone is happy wherever they end up. Vanderslice, 90, and Walsh are best for sophomore year. The Mods are where you live senior year."

The College Prowler Take On...
Campus Housing

The living arrangements at Boston College are very comfortable, mostly modern, and very well kept. The main downside to BC's housing is the fact that the freshman dorms have communal bathrooms. If you're one of those people who absolutely cannot shower with others while wearing flip-flops, then you might want to pick another school with newer dorms that offer private bathrooms. Having said that, you would be trading some truly unique architecture. BC's dorms offer less privacy because most of the buildings are old, but the flip side to that is that buildings are much more attractive and roomy than your average college dormitory. Also, gross as it may sound to have to share a bathroom with an entire floor, it is a good way to start making friends right off the bat.

The freshman dorms on Upper are the most desirable. They received a stellar remodeling job, so they're totally current and accommodating. Newton is still at the lower end of the Totem pole because it's quite far from main campus, so try to avoid that if you can. Sophomores will want to live in 90 or Vanderslice, since they are newer and nicer, but some of the best sophomore shindigs can be found late at night in Walsh Hall. Juniors typically live off campus or abroad. Seniors will want to live in the Mods (modular apartments), because they are the coolest thing going on campus, complete with their own individual backyards. Also, no senior should shy away from Voute or Gabelli, as they are gorgeous apartments and town houses. Edmonds only drawback is its quirky elevator, so try to live on the first floor if you can. Overall, BC maintains clean, safe, and enjoyable living quarters.

B

The College Prowler® Grade on
Campus Housing: B

A high Campus Housing grade indicates that dorms are clean, well-maintained, and spacious. Other determining factors include variety of dorms, proximity to classes, and social atmosphere.

www.collegeprowler.com

Off-Campus Housing

The Lowdown On...
Off-Campus Housing

Undergrads Living in Off-Campus Housing:

20%

Average Rent For:

Studio Apt.: $500–$600

1BR Apt.: $600–$800

2BR Apt.: $1,000–$1,300

Popular Areas:

Cleveland Circle

Commonwealth Avenue

Orkney

For Assistance Contact:

Boston College's Off-Campus Housing Office

www.bc.edu/offices/reslife/ offcampus

(617) 552-3075

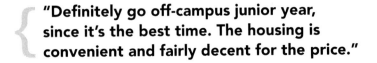

Students Speak Out On...
Off-Campus Housing

{ **"Definitely go off-campus junior year, since it's the best time. The housing is convenient and fairly decent for the price."**

Q "It's convenient as far as location. **The BC bus runs close to most of the popular spots for students to live off-campus**. Getting a good place is very competitive, though. During my junior year, I lived in a house and paid $600 a month plus utilities. I also had a parking spot."

Q "Boston is the land of apartments. My roommates and **I found one in like two days with a realtor**, but they're very expensive. There is no way to escape that. It's Boston. It's very easy to find an apartment, though, and they're close to campus. No one worries about finding one."

Q "**It's worth living off-campus**, if even for just a year. Most people have to move off because they are only given three years of on-campus housing. Start looking for places to live nine months before you want to live there, because it's a race."

Q "**A majority of BC juniors are forced to live off campus** for their entire junior year. Although this may sound like a major inconvenience on paper, it is truly a good learning experience, and something that the school is very involved with. It helps the BC overcrowded-housing issue, but also allows local rent prices to be ridiculously jacked up due to the supply/demand curve. If they charge it, you will have to come. Warning: don't live above restaurants unless you're really interested in getting up close and personal with a variety of daring rodents."

Q "**Living off-campus can be the greatest time**, if you get a good group of people. Try to find a place that has a dishwasher, because it can help with the cleaning arguments a lot. Places in Cleveland Circle are good, but also the 1700s of Commonwealth Avenue, Gerald, and Chiswick."

Q "Off-campus housing tends to be conveniently close to the campus, but can be difficult to find sometimes. **BC does not have any of its own off-campus housing**, so each student is on their own to find an off-campus residence. However, there never seems to be a big problem with off-campus housing. Most students live in Cleveland Circle, which is about a mile and half down the road."

Q "People generally **live off campus or go abroad during their junior year, then come back to campus for their senior year.** It's a hassle to find an apartment and live off campus, but everyone does it. You just live in one of the nearby neighborhoods if you don't go abroad."

Q "Usually freshmen, sophomores, and seniors live on campus. Most people, unless they are in the top five percent of the incoming class, a nursing student or a varsity athlete, are only given three years of on-campus housing. So, **juniors usually live off campus up and down Commonwealth Avenue** and on the little side streets. Apartments are very expensive."

Q "If you only get three years of housing, then in your junior year you have to look for off-campus housing. It can be a pain, but usually everything works out and you find housing with or without help from BC. **I heard that sometimes living off campus can be cheaper than living on campus** if you know how to do it right and find good deals."

Q "**Juniors typically live off campus**, which is where most of the really cool parties are besides the Mods. I'll be living off campus next year and I am really looking forward to it."

Q "Really, only juniors live off campus. Most people only get three years of housing because there just isn't enough room on campus. But it's really convenient. All of the juniors live right down Commonwealth Avenue and there's a bus that comes by about every 10 minutes. Personally, **I can't wait to live off campus** and get to throw all the parties."

Q "Pretty much all of the areas surrounding campus are occupied by students. The only downside though is that **it's pretty expensive**."

Q "Off-campus housing is very convenient. There is a shuttle bus that runs through the major sections of town where BC students live, and **you can usually find nice, affordable housing**. However, most students prefer to live on campus for all four years, so if you can get four years of housing, take it."

Q "I live off campus now and I like it so much better than living on campus, but **it is really expensive**. When you break it down though, it can be cheaper than paying BC for housing depending on how much the rent is per month."

The College Prowler Take On...
Off-Campus Housing

Boston College simply does not have enough allocated housing to accommodate all of its students. Most students are given only three years of housing, so living off campus becomes a necessity. If you are one of those students, then the best advice I can give you is to plan ahead. Start looking for an apartment early. The longer you put off looking, the harder it will be. You will certainly be able to find an apartment no matter what, but the cheapest apartments are the ones that get taken first. You will literally pay the price if you procrastinate. Having an apartment in Boston can be extremely expensive, as you usually have to pay for so much more than you bargained for, like maintenance. You might also want to make sure that the people you're living with are responsible enough to have an apartment. No one wants to live with someone who's constantly late with the rent or sticks you with the whole electric bill.

Some students are given four years of housing, which is truly a convenient asset. However, many individuals love living off campus, as it gives them a dose of city living and quasi-adult behavior. The extra freedom and responsibility of moving off campus can be a great experience, if you're ready for it. Furthermore, you can always sidestep the off-campus housing obstacle by going abroad for an alternative experience. It's kind of unfortunate that those are the only two options available to students: living off campus or going abroad. But that is what happens when you go to school in a big city; the school just doesn't have space to house every student.

B+

The College Prowler® Grade on

Off-Campus
Housing: B+

A high grade in Off-Campus Housing indicates that apartments are of high quality, close to campus, affordable, and easy to secure.

Diversity

The Lowdown On...
Diversity

Native American:
Less than 1%

White:
76%

Asian American:
9%

International:
2%

African American:
6%

Out-of-State:
72%

Hispanic:
7%

Political Activity

Students are politically active on both the Republican and Democratic side, although more students are Republicans with the school being as conservative as it is.

Gay Pride

There are a couple organizations on campus, but only one, Allies of Boston College, is recognized by the school and its constitution states that it is there to provide support, but not advocacy. It is very much rooted in Catholic beliefs, and is really just a place to discuss sexuality. Another organization, the Lesbian, Gay, and Bisexual Community (LGBC), is a more active, liberally minded organization, but it has repeatedly been denied status as a recognized student organization. Still, they are active on campus. Most students are tolerant of the gay, lesbian, bisexual, and transsexual community, but as a whole, BC isn't incredibly welcoming towards people with sexual orientations other than heterosexual.

Economic Status

Most students are middle- to upper-class.

Minority Clubs

AHANA, an acronym to describe individuals of African-American, Hispanic, Asian, or Native American descent, is a student group that, for over 20 years, has implemented programs to foster the diversity at Boston College. From extracurricular to academic, AHANA makes a huge impact on the lives of all students at BC. There are also other organizations on campus specifically for certain cultures or nationalities.

Students Speak Out On...
Diversity

> **"Sadly, this campus is not all that diverse. Though BC is trying desperately to diversify, it's probably my least favorite aspect of this school. It's not a very accepting and open minded campus, either."**

Q "**Diverse enough**, but everyone can tend to look the same."

Q "**Some days it can feel like everyone at BC dresses the same**, hails from the same type of background and wants to take similar paths in life. However, there are those moments when you meet someone from a completely different upbringing than your own, and has a totally unique perspective on life. Unfortunately, most of those moments occur when speaking with a stranger while you're travelling abroad in Germany."

Q "The problem with BC is that, since **there aren't many minorities represented** on campus right now, not many minorities are going to want to come to Chestnut Hill and be one of the few exceptions to the typical BC student. It's the chicken and the egg problem."

Q "I thought Boston College was **plenty diverse**. I didn't really find any problems with it."

Q "**Boston College is trying to make the atmosphere more diverse and attractive to minorities**. If the administration can fix this major problem in the next few years, little else needs to be addressed to make BC an almost perfect school."

Q "Students that come from different nations end up hanging out mostly with only students from their home countries. You could go through all four years of school and never know that someone from Puerto Rico or another country went to BC as well. **It can get pretty cliquey at BC**, but that's probably expected."

Q "I would say that most of the students are white, but it's not like there aren't any non-white students. **There is a group called AHANA, which is essentially all of the non-white students**. You are signed up for it automatically if your application says you aren't white."

Q "**Boston College is not very diverse**. *The Princeton Review* voted BC the most homogeneous college in the country. I've never witnessed or experienced any racism, though."

Q "There's not much diversity in comparison with other colleges. But **we do have people of all races** and religions. In fact, my roommate was from Korea. There's less diversity at BC than at most other colleges but that's mainly because it's a Jesuit institution. However, you do not have to be religious to go to this school and you do not have to go to church. There are clubs where different groups gather and share their common background. Usually people integrate."

Q "**It's not the most diverse campus**, but every year it gets better. We broke the record for the most AHANA students ever in one class this year, and I'm sure next year's class will break it again."

The College Prowler Take On...
Diversity

Cultivating a more diverse student body at Boston College may currently be the school's largest problem. The majority of students are Caucasian and middle- to upper-class. Walking across campus, that's probably all you'll see. A lot of students feel that it's not the school's fault that many of the people it attracts hail from similar backgrounds. Yet, BC is diligently working towards drawing individuals from different upbringings and social demographics, and the other students are becoming more accepting and inclusive of what diversity it does have. Hopefully, this will help increase BC's diversity in the future.

Overall, the school is aware of the lack of diversity on campus and is working to rectify the problem. Many students are not the least bit uncomfortable with the demographics represented at the school; others may press the issue. Potential students should recognize the social landscape before they decide to attend Boston College. Nonetheless, you really have to prepare yourself for a sea of pea coats in the fall and J. Crew skirts in the spring. It's a very preppy campus. Once again, there are exceptions to this rule, but you have to search for diversity. Some people thrive in the fairly homogenous atmosphere while others detest it, but the mixed bag is hopefully becoming more assorted.

The College Prowler® Grade on

Diversity: D-

A high grade in Diversity indicates that ethnic minorities and international students have a notable presence on campus and that students of different economic backgrounds, religious beliefs, and sexual preferences are well-represented.

Guys & Girls

The Lowdown On...
Guys & Girls

Men Undergrads:	Women Undergrads:
47%	53%

Birth Control Available?

Because of the religious affiliation of the college, University Health Services does not provide birth control to students.

Social Scene

The social scene at Boston College can be difficult to navigate for the first couple of years. On-campus drinking can be impossible, with the BCPD making their stern presence known loud and clear. Students don't want to run the risk of getting written up or getting slapped with housing probation that can shadow a student throughout his entire academic career. Boston College doesn't encourage drinking, and it certainly doesn't foster or tolerate underage drinking. Needless to say, many students find a way to play hard anyway.

Hookups or Relationships?

Hookups are way more popular since most of us are just looking to have fun. If you're looking for a relationship, chances are you'll be able to find other people that are, too, but it's definitely easier to just date around.

Best Place to Meet Guys/Girls

Mary Ann's. Descriptions of the place range from "a fun dive bar" to "a disgusting health-code violation," but one thing most students agree upon is that it's a perfect place to meet young, BC-attending members of the opposite sex.

Dress Code

The dress code at Boston College is widely known as preppy. At times, it can seem that BC is the sole entity that keeps Abercrombie & Fitch in business. Many women like to dress up and show off their cute new outfits for class, whereas only a few guys bring out their exclusive wardrobes for an 11 a.m. seminar. Sweats and fleeces make appearances in many a class, especially the courses that start at 9 a.m. However, when asked, many BC students could care less about their appearance. It is always refreshing that the student body isn't entirely filled with Barbie and Ken dolls.

Did You Know?

Top Places to Find Hotties:

1. The Plex
2. On the way to class
3. Mod parties

Students Speak Out On...
Guys & Girls

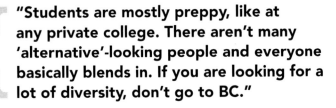

"Students are mostly preppy, like at any private college. There aren't many 'alternative'-looking people and everyone basically blends in. If you are looking for a lot of diversity, don't go to BC."

Q "We have a beautiful campus, and I'm not talking about the gothic buildings. **I personally believe the guys are hotter than the girls**. BC isn't really a dating school, though. There are so many really attractive people that most people tend not to settle down and seriously date. That's not to say that I don't know a few couples, but there are many more single people running around than non-singles."

Q "**A lot of lookers at BC**! Most people look the same, but there are plenty of stand-out hotties."

Q "The girls are super hot, but on the whole, the guys look immature and scrawny. **It is definitely uneven**!"

Q "**A high emphasis is placed on appearance at BC**, so many people just use whatever they have been blessed with to the best of their ability. It seems like no one really experiments with looks, so if you have originality, you could definitely stand out on campus, for better or worse!"

Q "Guys can be ridiculously short, and **the girls can be super thin**. Those are the common extremes."

Q "I would say that **the typical BC student is a little spoiled and quite sociable**, though my views might be a little skewed. I know that many of the girls are blonde and fit the preppy stereotype, and many are pretty nice."

Q "There are groups of preppy students, classy students, athletic students, etc. Everybody is usually really nice, but cliques do form. There are definitely **a lot of good looking guys**, but there are also a lot of pretty girls."

Q "I personally think that **we have a good-looking population**. There are lots of pretty girls and the guys aren't too shabby either. It does seem like everyone has the same look, though. The girls are all into J. Crew and Abercrombie, and a lot of the guys have come from private, Catholic, preppy schools, so most of them are boring dressers, too."

Q "**The chicks here are hot, and there are more girls than guys**. BC is a very fit place, so you don't see many overweight people here. On average, I think both the guys and the girls at BC are better looking than the ones at a lot of other schools that I have visited."

Q "**A lot of BC girls are workout-aholics**. There are a lot of really thin girls walking around."

Q "Guys are decent. The hot ones are your typical frat/prep/ jock types. **Many of the girls are practically identical**: preppy, rich, beautiful."

Q "Everyone looks the same for the most part. **Girls are very fit and are usually perfectionists**. Guys are usually of average height, and have little fashion sense. There is even something called a 'BC haircut' that guys can receive at local barber shops. It's just a basic short cut with spiky bangs."

Q "**There are a lot of good looking people on campus**. Most of the people are kind of preppy. There are lots of blonde-haired, blue-eyed Irish girls which can get kind of annoying. Being a brunette, you actually stand out at BC, which works for me. Honestly, sometimes I don't even like going to parties at other schools because I know the guys won't be as good-looking, and I'm so picky when I go home now. I love my BC boys."

Q "**There are a lot of beautiful, rich people**, but everyone is very nice. I've met a lot of really cool people who have become some of my best friends."

Q "The people at BC are pretty nice in general. There are some who are a little stuck on themselves, but you'll find that everywhere. **The guys are hot**! Sometimes it does feel like people just stepped out of a J. Crew catalog because a lot of girls put a lot of effort into their looks. During the winter, though, everyone just wants to keep warm, so it doesn't really matter what you wear."

The College Prowler Take On...
Guys & Girls

Overall, Boston College is a remarkably attractive campus, although very homogenous. The girls are typically gorgeous (if by gorgeous you mean blonde, thin, wealthy, and super smart). On the other hand, several students commented that BC guys, for whatever reason, are short and not very socially adept, though there are a few notable exceptions to this rule. Most students place a lot of emphasis on appearance, for better or for worse, so be prepared. This is not the kind of place where you walk around in ripped jeans and flip flops or come to class still in your pajamas. In some ways it's nice that everyone makes such an effort to look presentable, but it can also put pressure on you to look just as nice, even when you have an early class and stayed up all night finishing a paper.

The overall image for both sexes is a fairly preppy, Abercrombie & Fitch or J. Crew look. Most people on campus fit that description. There are people with other styles on campus, but they are few and far between. It might be a little overwhelming, for example, to walk around campus with a mohawk. Nobody would give you a hard time, but you might get some weird looks or become known as "the person with the mohawk" because you'd stand out so much. In short, you can dress or look however you want to, but you might be a little intimidated by how similar everyone else is.

The College Prowler® Grade on
Guys: B+

A high grade for Guys indicates that the male population on campus is attractive, smart, friendly, and engaging, and that the school has a decent ratio of guys to girls.

The College Prowler® Grade on
Girls: A

A high grade for Girls not only implies that the women on campus are attractive, smart, friendly, and engaging, but also that there is a fair ratio of girls to guys.

Athletics

The Lowdown On...
Athletics

Athletic Division:
Division I-A

Conference:
ACC

Athletic Fields:
Shea Field

School Mascot:
Eagle

Males Playing Varsity Sports:
8%

Females Playing Varsity Sports:
7%

➜

Men's Varsity Sports:

Baseball

Basketball

Cross Country

Fencing

Football

Golf

Ice Hockey

Sailing

Skiing

Soccer

Swimming and Diving

Tennis

Track and Field

Women's Varsity Sports:

Basketball

Cross Country

Fencing

Field Hockey

Golf

Ice Hockey

Lacrosse

Rowing

Sailing

Skiing

Soccer

Softball

Swimming and Diving

Tennis

Track and Field

Volleyball

Club Sports:

Cheerleading

Crew

Cycling

Karate

Lacrosse

Rugby

Soccer

Ultimate Frisbee

Volleyball

Skiing and Snowboarding

Field Hockey

Water Polo

Intramurals:

Men's:

Basketball

Ice Hockey

Racquetball

Softball

Squash

Tennis

Touch Football

Volleyball

Women's:

Basketball

Ice Hockey

Racquetball

Tennis

Volleyball

Getting Tickets

You will need tickets to go to the games, and almost everyone gets season tickets. To buy tickets, call (617) 552-GoBC.

Most Popular Sports

Football, basketball

Best Place to Take a Walk

Quad or around Conte Forum

Gyms/Facilities

Flynn Recreation Complex

The Flynn "Rex Plex" contains two pools, a heated spa, an indoor track, tennis courts, basketball courts, volleyball courts, and racquetball/squash courts.

Students Speak Out On...
Athletics

"Club sports and intramural sports have a pretty good following. I played rugby all four years and I was captain my senior year. It was one of the most fun things I did at BC."

Q "Varsity sports are massive at BC. There are over 800 varsity athletes at Boston College! **The only varsity sports that are considered big are football, basketball, hockey, and lately soccer and field hockey**. Intramural sports are considerable as well. On the day of intramural sign ups, people get to the office to get in line at 9 a.m. and sign-ups don't start until 4 p.m."

Q "Everyone supports the sports teams, especially the hockey, football and basketball teams. If you get the chance, definitely **buy season tickets to at least hockey and football games**. You won't regret it! Even if you're not a big sports person, sporting events are crazy social events from which you'll have some of the best memories ever."

Q "Varsity sports are a huge part of BC life because we are a Division I school. **Football games are a big deal, with tailgating all across campus**. Hockey is also huge, as we have graced the Frozen Four with our presence often. All other sports also do very well. We have a range of sports, from the above-stated to crew, fencing, and wrestling. IM sports are also major, as many students participate in them, but they do not draw fans like the varsity sports do."

Q "Boston College is a very sports-oriented school. **Football games in the fall are a big event**. Get tickets! You'll want them because that's how most of your Saturdays will be spent. I don't even really like football that much, but I like going to the games. We're a Division I Big East school, so sports are a part of life here. Our hockey team won the national championship and the men's and women's basketball teams won the Big East tournaments. To sum it up, sports are a big deal. That's not to say that you can't avoid them, because you can. But if you're interested in sports, you picked the right place."

Q "**The sports at BC are enormous**. The BC sports scene could rival any other school in the nation."

Q "**A lot of the social life centers around the sports teams**. Our big rivalry weekend, when we play against Notre Dame in football and hockey, is our biggest party weekend of the year."

Q "Make sure you get season tickets for football, hockey and basketball games. Even if you can't go to a game, someone will buy the ticket from you. Everyone goes to games. My freshman year, I didn't have tickets and felt very left out when everyone I knew was at the football game. **IM sports are big, too**. There are lots of sports to choose from and lots of people join them."

Q "**Everyone goes to the football games and they are usually all-day events**. The other games are really fun as well. There are a bunch of IM sports including Frisbee, rugby, basketball, and softball which seem to be pretty popular."

Q "Varsity sports are huge. Football games are huge in the fall. You tailgate first, go to the game, go home and nap for a while, and then go to a party. **Everyone has a party after a football game**. The rest of the sports are pretty big too, especially basketball and hockey, although I didn't really get into them. I'm not a big sports fan."

The College Prowler Take On...
Athletics

Sports are huge at BC! Football, basketball and hockey are the big three sports at BC, and pretty much everyone is in tune to how the teams are doing. Tailgating for football games is the highlight of many BC students' experiences. Here, alumni, parents, and students run rampant through campus on the morning of the game, enjoying fall, food, and flavored beer. The spirit in the stadium is palpable and a total rush for any sports fan. BC prides itself on its athletic program, so you're bound to catch a solid basketball, hockey or football season. Lesser known sports excel, but don't receive the same attention the big three do. Intramural sports are also major at BC, with hundreds of people lining up on sign-up day for spots on the teams. Word to the wise: get there early, or you could lose your chance at playing!

If you're not into sports, BC might not be a great place for you. You certainly don't have to get into sports, but you might feel a little left out as everyone revs up for game day and you don't really care. There's always the other option of going to the games just to hang out with people, which can be fun and doesn't require actually knowing the rules or caring about sports.

The College Prowler® Grade on

Athletics: A

A high grade in Athletics indicates that students have school spirit, that sports programs are respected, that games are well-attended, and that intramurals are a prominent part of student life.

Nightlife

The Lowdown On...
Nightlife

Club and Bar Prowler: Popular Nightlife Spots!

Club Prowler:

There are lots of clubs in Boston, and many of them are open to people 18 and over, making going to clubs one of the only kinds of nightlife freshmen can have.

Avalon

15 Lansdowne Street
Boston, MA
(617) 262-2424

Avalon, one of Boston's most popular clubs, plays primarily top 40 and tehcno, with occasional live music. Sunday nights are gay/lesbian nights.

Axis

13 Lansdowne Street
Boston, MA
(617) 262-2437

Right next to Avalon, Axis is just as popular with a slightly younger crowd (19+).

➜

Bar Prowler:

There are tons of bars around campus and in Boston. For upperclassmen, these are the places to be pretty much every night of the week. Everyone has a personal favorite, but BC students agree that most of them are a really good time.

The Avenue Bar & Grill

1249 Commonwealth Ave.

Allston, MA 02134

(617) 782-9508

The Avenue is a bar and restaurant; it's not too trendy and upscale, but the food, though good, can get expensive. The beer selection is considerable, with a few imports and microbews you're not likely to find elsewhere.

Big City

138 Brighton Ave.

Allston, MA 02134

(617) 728-2020

Big City is a bar and pool hall decked out to resemble a 1950s police station. The bar offers a very respectable beer selection, and pool is free from 6 p.m.–8 p.m.

Great Scott's

1222 Commonwealth Ave.

Allston, MA 02134

(617) 734-4502

A popular college bar, Great Scott's has a dance floor, though dancing isn't as much the focus here as it is at some

(Great Scott's, continued)

of Boston's clubs. Wednesday nights, which are ladies' nights, are big at Scott's.

The Kinvara Irish Pub

34 Harvard Ave.

Allston, MA 02134

(617) 783-9400

www.kinvaraboston.com

A mix between a lounge, a dance bar, and a sports bar, Kinvara also regularly hosts darts and trivia competitions.

Mary Ann's

1937 Beacon St.

Boston, MA 02135

Mary Ann's is a college dive in the best sense of the word. All of the finances not wasted on decor or keeping the place clean are instead funneled into keeping the beer cheap, making Mary Ann's not only the most popular BC hangout, but also the cheapest place around to get a drink.

T's Pub

973 Commonwealth Ave.

Boston, MA 02215

(617) 254-0807

T's is more of a Boston University hangout than a BC one, which makes sense, given that it's dead in the middle of BU's west campus. It's a typical college bar; it's crowded, inexpensive, and offers a decent beer selection.

Tonic

1316 Commonwealth Ave

Allston, MA 02134

(617) 566-6699

Part bar, part lounge, Tonic is somewhat more upscale than many of its neighbors; the food and mixed drinks are good, though expensive. The downstairs lounge is typically a little quieter and less crowded than the rest of the bar if you're looking to relax.

Wonderbar

186 Harvard Ave.

Allston, MA

(617) 351-COOL

Wonderbar is a trendy, upscale lounge and restaurant. It's certainly more expensive than a lot of other local bars, but it's a nice change of scenery from the more college-oriented establishments.

Other Places to Check Out:

Axis, CitySide Bar & Grille, The Green Briar, Joey's, The Kells, The Last Drop, Roggie's, Who's on First

Useful Resources for Nightlife:

www.boston.com

Bars Close At:

Most bars close at 1 or 2 a.m

Primary Areas with Nightlife:

Harvard Avenue, Faneuil Hall

Cheapest Place to Get a Drink:

Mary Ann's

Student Favorites:

CitySide, Roggie's, Mary Ann's

Favorite Drinking Games:

Beirut, Century Club, Flip Cup, Power Hour, Quarters

Organization Parties

There aren't many organization parties on campus, although we do have our share of house parties, which are very popular and always a good time.

Frats

See the Greek section!

Students Speak Out On...
Nightlife

"On-campus parties aren't very fun unless they are before or after football games, or during senior week. There is a ton of bars and clubs off-campus. You can always find a place you like, like Mary Ann's, CitySide, Tonic, Avalon, Roggie's, or Who's on First."

Q "The bars and clubs are good. **Mary Ann's is a bar within walking distance** where most students hangout and there is whole section of Boston behind Fenway that is mostly just bars and clubs."

Q "There are tons of clubs! There are streets that are lined with bars and clubs which range from sports bars to dance to goth to techno to pool, and anything else you can imagine. **Some of the best spots are Lansdowne Street** and by Fanueil Hall."

Q "**There are always a million parties going on**, so if you're willing to search, you'll never be bored. Freshmen can't have parties because the RAs are always on duty, but from sophomore year on, you can do what you want. Most of the good parties are off campus in the junior apartments. Once you go to a few, you'll have an in to all the other parties at that apartment for the year."

Q "**Upperclassmen start the weekend on Tuesday night**, usually at Mary Ann's. The line can start as early as 10 p.m., so get there early. Happy hour at MA's is big on Friday afternoons. Thursdays are usually somewhere on Harvard Avenue."

Q "Bars can be super **strict at the beginning of each semester**, but usually let up later on. Be careful for random raids!"

Q "**A majority of people do drink at BC since it's college**, but there are also a lot of people who just aren't into that scene. It's not like you have to drink to have fun on the weekends. There are always alternatives: a cappella concerts, plays, dance shows, excursions in Boston, etc. We're not isolated in the middle of the woods sitting around with nothing to do but drink."

Q "**There are plenty of bars up and down Commonwealth Avenue**, one of the main roads of the city, all of which are accessible via the T or a five-minute taxi cab ride. As far as clubs are concerned, you do have to venture further into the city to get to them, normally via cab, but once you're in the city there are many different club choices, and there are some 18-and-over nights."

Q "The White Horse was a frequent watering hole, as was Kinvara, the Avenue, Great Scott's, and even Tonic towards the end of my college career. **CitySide isn't bad, it's just that the bar is too big for the room**, so people can get really crowded."

Q "**Go to T's for karaoke**! It's the best on Tuesday nights."

Q "The club scene is really fun. **Avalon Street is the place to go**. The bars are fun too, but you need a pretty good ID and some backup to get into them. Some bars are known as 'BC bars' and are somewhat easier to get into, especially on Wednesday and Thursday nights. Kinvara, Great Scott's, and Wonderbar are the more popular ones that we go to."

Q "Most **clubs are either 19-and-over or 21-and-over on the weekends**, but you can get into most clubs if you're 18 on Thursdays, so don't schedule early Friday classes."

Q "I'm more of a bar girl than a club girl. **I love the bar scene at BC**: Kinvara, my personal favorite and a BC hangout, has dancing and drinking and is generally a great time. Great Scott's, another good one, is kind of like Kinvara and Wonderbar, which is a more upscale and dressy jazz bar. Big City is okay, but there are so many more."

Q "**On Lansdowne Street there are about a billion clubs and bars**. It's very easy and very cheap to get there by cab or on the T."

Q "Practically everyone goes to a club during their first month of school and then many people keep going every Thursday when it's 18-and-over night. Bars are a bit more complicated since an MIT student died a few years back from alcohol poisoning. Everyone in Boston is incredibly strict about that whole scene and the Boston cops have really cracked down on it. **One would need a really good fake ID to get into some spots**, but most bars now scan IDs, so you would have to have a real license. I haven't gotten to go to a bar yet."

The College Prowler Take On...
Nightlife

Freshmen and sophomores can have a hard time finding quality parties at BC. The BCPD crack down pretty hard on underage drinking, so dorm parties don't really happen. Once you're 21, though, a new world can open up to you. Mary Ann's is the local watering hole where everyone goes for a beer, and CitySide and Roggie's come up as close contenders. Harvard Avenue is only a $10 cab ride or a cheap T ride away, and boasts six or seven mediocre to fairly great bars for the average Joe.

Big spenders can hit up downtown, where a cab can cost you anywhere between 20 and 30 bucks. Definitely fill up the cab with all of your pals so you can split the costs. Fanieul Hall has literally hundreds of great spots, but you probably won't run into anyone you know other than people you came with—which can be refreshing some nights! No matter what you are looking to do, you'll be able to find it somewhere.

A

The College Prowler® Grade on
Nightlife: A

A high grade in Nightlife indicates that there are many bars and clubs in the area that are easily accessible and affordable. Other determining factors include the number of options for the under-21 crowd and the prevalence of house parties.

Greek Life

The Lowdown On...
Greek Life

Number of Fraternities:
0

Number of Sororities:
0

Students Speak Out On...
Greek Life

{ **"There is no Greek life at Boston College. I like to think that it's because we all just party together!"**

Q "There are no fraternities and sororities on campus. At first, I wasn't happy about this, but now that I'm older the idea of cliques like sororities seems really stupid. Socially at BC there are no 'cool' groups and no social hierarchies, which is **a nice change from high school**."

Q "There is no Greek life. **Jesuit schools don't have fraternities or sororities**. There are, however, plenty of off-campus parties to make up for that. Just walk up Commonwealth Avenue and you'll find plenty of parties, most of which you can just walk into and pay five dollars for a plastic cup for the keg."

Q "We do not have frats or sororities, which I love. **No one is 'cooler' or 'better' than anyone else**, it's a really even social scene. And it's not like we don't still have raging parties!"

Q "**There is no Greek life at all at BC**. I really like this and I think that most other people here would agree. There are parties on and off campus, but not having different houses and rushing is definitely good."

Q "**Boston College doesn't have any fraternities** because it's a Catholic school and we're not allowed. But don't worry; we still have a good time. Most all of the juniors live off campus so they're always having parties, and I've been to quite a few frat parties at other schools around BC like Tufts and BU, and honestly, I wasn't that impressed. They're crowded, the people are trashy, and the guys are sleazy. We also have a huge emphasis on sports, so the teams, which are kind of our mini-version of frats, have parties a lot. Seniors that live on campus have good parties in the Mods, which is also a great to tailgate before football games—another huge part of BC social life."

The College Prowler Take On...
Greek Life

The lack of a Greek life on-campus will most likely not affect your overall experience at BC (unless you are into that sort of thing). At times, it can feel like there is a Greek life, especially if you take into consideration the Newton Campus versus Upper Campus allegiances and rivalries. Students from these two sections of campus can get inexplicably territorial.

Nevertheless, not having a Greek life is a positive asset of BC in many ways. Cliquish behavior, paying dues, and hazing are not areas BC, or any school for that matter, are in desperate need of fulfilling. Social interaction and mixing with groups should be encouraged, and Greek life, at times, runs the risk of alienating individuals.

N/A

The College Prowler® Grade on
Greek Life: N/A

A high grade in Greek Life indicates that sororities and fraternities are not only present, but also active on campus. Other determining factors include the variety of houses available and the respect the Greek community receives from the rest of the campus.

Drug Scene

The Lowdown On...
Drug Scene

Most Prevalent Drugs on Campus:

Alcohol

Marijuana

Liquor-Related Referrals:

0

Liquor-Related Arrests:

38

Drug-Related Referrals:

0

Drug-Related Arrests:

1

Drug Counseling Programs

Alcohol and Drug Education is a service run by the Office of the Dean for Student Development. This program helps students do personal assessments and find referral programs when necessary. They also help students find support groups or 12-step programs. For more information, go to *www.bc.edu/offices/ade.*

Students Speak Out On...
Drug Scene

> "Police are overly strict concerning alcohol. They treat it like manslaughter, but they brush all drug violations under the rug, which is mighty convenient for the growing number of cokeheads on campus."

Q "**You can't miss pot**, and I've seen coke a few times. You can probably find most drugs if you look hard enough."

Q "**People drink at BC**. I have never even seen drug use since I arrived."

Q "The only hard drug use I have seen is marijuana, if that is even considered hard. **BC isn't a drug school**, it's a drinking school. Work hard, play hard."

Q "**The drug scene is not really big**, although it depends on who you hang out with. If people are doing drugs, they're usually just smoking. Drinking is a much more popular activity."

Q "Drinking is big, but **most drugs are looked down upon by the students**, except for pot."

Q "**There's weed if you know who to go to**, and there are some kids who do 'shrooms and coke."

Q "**There's the usual amount of weed on campus**. I'm not sure about the hard stuff, but I don't know anybody who does those things. There are a couple of people who roll sometimes, but other than that it's not prominent enough to notice."

Q "**The hardest thing I've seen on campus is weed**, though I'm sure that there are people doing harder things."

Q "Drinking is very heavy but can be avoided. For drugs, **marijuana is the most common** I think, but cocaine, E, mushrooms, and anything that one can snort can also be found, but all of these can also be avoided."

The College Prowler Take On...
Drug Scene

Alcohol is where it's at for BC. Whether it's house parties, the bar or football games, people on campus love to drink. It can be difficult when you're under 21, because it seems like everyone is drinking but you, which might not be that far from the truth. The BCPD is very strict about underage drinking, so you really are taking a major risk every time you drink on campus if you're not of age. Once you turn 21, though, there is suddenly so much more going on. Pretty much everyone drinks on campus, so get your drinking hat on. If you don't drink, you'll be able to find other people to hang out with, but you might feel a little like an outsider.

The illicit drug scene is not at all out in the open. It fluctuates in its popularity, but is usually very quiet and not center-stage (as alcohol is). While there are definitely people to see and places to go for any kind of drug under the sun, this type of activity isn't usually popular with the majority of students. It's there if you want it, but you can certainly avoid it if you're not interested. Boston College administration and security officers are not tolerant of drugs. The school and its officials do not condone drug use of any kind, under any circumstances. Most students are afraid of the repercussions of not only the physical harm to their bodies, but also from the school administration if ever convicted of drug use. All in all, the drug scene is pretty tame. The alcohol scene, though, is a little more present.

B+

The College Prowler® Grade on
Drug Scene: B+

A high grade in the Drug Scene indicates that drugs are not a noticeable part of campus life; drug use is not visible, and no pressure to use them seems to exist.

Campus
Strictness

The Lowdown On...
Campus Strictness

What Are You Most Likely to Get Caught Doing on Campus?
- Underage drinking
- Drugs
- Being rowdy

Students Speak Out On...
Campus Strictness

"What you can get away with really depends on your RA. Mine was great so we got away with murder, but I know some others who really weren't cool at all. "

Q "The police force can be pretty strict about underage drinking and drug use. **First-time offenders get a letter sent home** and second- and third-time offenders are in danger of losing their housing. It's pretty serious if you get caught, so my best advice is to do everything discreetly and not to be obnoxious about it. If you're going to drink then drink, but don't start advertising keg parties in your room. You will get busted!"

Q "As with any law enforcement agency, the BCPD frown upon the use of illegal drugs and underage drinking. Ball up, be smart, and **you can get away with mass-murder**."

Q "Pretty much everyone has some story about the BCPD and have some level of annoyance regarding the offense. **It all depends on the altercation**, but usually they are standard irritating pain in the butts."

Q "I've heard of a few stories where students were just completely stupid and pulled some kind of stunt that warranted the severe punishment they received. **The administration is not out to ruin your life**, but if you make foolish mistakes, the higher-ups will let you have it!"

Q "**Campus police are extremely strict on drugs**. If you're caught with marijuana, you will most likely be thrown out. They aren't too strict about drinking but they're not lenient. If you get caught drinking you will get some sort of punishment. By your second or third punishment you will most likely be told to live off-campus for the next semester, or to take AA classes. If a BCPD officer sees you extremely drunk on campus, he will take you to St. Elizabeth's hospital for the night. Your parents and the school will be notified and you will get in trouble. I haven't found this campus too strict with drinking, though."

Q "Your ability to drink and have a good time on campus can somewhat be determined by the coolness of your RA. If you get stuck with a lame one, you'll have to trek to your friends dorms where they have more relaxed RAs. **Some care about noise and partying, some don't**. It's luck of the draw."

Q "BC is kind of known as a drinking school. **There aren't many drugs just because everyone drinks so much**. But drugs are there to some extent; I guess it just depends on who you hang out with, like it would anywhere. I've never gotten in trouble for drinking or anything, but they aren't exactly lenient. I mean, if you get caught very obviously drunk, you'll probably get in trouble, and if you get caught in the act of drinking, you'll probably get in trouble as well, unless you're somewhere where seniors live because they're 21, like the Mods. Off campus at the junior's parties you don't get in trouble either."

Q "**It's not too hard to get liquor or to drink it**. I guess you just can't be too obvious about it. Don't walk around campus stumbling because the police will take you to the infirmary and write you up. And if you're in your room don't be too crazy. But how crazy you can be all depends on your RA."

Q "**There are fairly strict policies on drugs and alcohol**, especially in freshman dorms, and they'll try to scare you with it at orientation and stuff, but it's nothing that you can't get around, so I wouldn't worry."

Q "The police are semi-strict. **I drink every weekend and have never been caught**, but I know plenty who have been. It's all a matter of luck. And the first time they catch you, it's not bad at all, just a letter home. I think it's a 'three strikes and you're out of housing' policy, but there are always parties on and off campus that never get busted."

The College Prowler Take On...
Campus Strictness

The BCPD are definitely strict about underage drinking and drug use, so you'll have to learn the ropes if you ever want to participate in the social scene. However, "work hard, play hard" is an unofficial BC motto, so serious fun certainly can and does occur. The first few months of every semester are always deemed "lock down," where the PD goes overboard in the strictness department. Usually it tapers off after a couple of weeks, so sit tight and drink quietly in your room. Keep the Beirut tournaments at a less than audible level, watch out for RAs and try not to make any foolish mistakes.

The campus usually maintains a level of strictness not unlike that of a federal penitentiary. (Well, not quite that strict, but you get the picture.) Truthfully, the school recognizes how hard Boston College students work in their academic life and how much the students like to reward themselves for their efforts in their personal lives. BCPD cracks down on drinking as much as they can, but historically, young people will always find a way to "play hard." You won't find many BC students running through campus drunk and naked at any hour of the day, but a good party can always be found at some locale during the week. Students who are willing to search for personal enjoyment usually find a just compensation.

The College Prowler® Grade on

Campus Strictness: C

A high Campus Strictness grade implies an overall lenient atmosphere; police and RAs are fairly tolerant, and the administration's rules are flexible.

Parking

The Lowdown On...
Parking

BC Parking Services:
Boston College
Parking and Traffic Office
Rubenstein Hall
Chestnut Hill, MA 02467
Telephone: (617) 552-4443

Common Parking Tickets:
Expired Meter: $25
No Parking Zone: $50
Handicapped Zone: $100

Student Parking Lot?
None

Freshmen Allowed to Park?
No

Parking Permit Cost:
$200

Did You Know?

Best Places to Find a Parking Spot

Parking Garage during the weekend, but not during football weekends. Cummington Street or Bay State Road, there are some open spots. Also, the further away from central campus, the easier it is to park; check down by Kenmore Square.

Good Luck Getting a Parking Spot Here!

Pretty much anywhere during the week.

Parking Permits

Permits are available through Student Services. You are not guaranteed a permit, and a permit does not guarantee you a space.

Students Speak Out On...
Parking

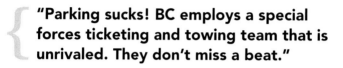

"Parking sucks! BC employs a special forces ticketing and towing team that is unrivaled. They don't miss a beat."

Q "**There is no parking on BC's campus**. Don't fool yourself. If you want to bring a car, you're out of luck. Finding legal parking at BC is like finding a scandalous girl on Friday night. Sometimes the cards are just stacked against you."

Q "If you have a parking pass, (which unless you're a nursing student, you probably won't) you can park on campus. Otherwise, you can still park, with the risk of getting a ticket, or getting towed. There is no overnight parking, except on weekends (and again, if you have that special pass). I brought my car up my senior year and found places around campus to park it, but there are a lot of times when you need to move it for whatever reason, and **it can become a pain to get to your car**, especially in the winter."

Q "I am always amazed when I hear about other college's ability to let students keep cars on campus. **It's just totally inconceivable to have a car at BC**. Although, it's not totally the school's fault. We are located near a major city so it's not like there is a ton of room for cars anyway."

Q "You can find businesses around Chestnut Hill, like Maddies Market, where you can pay for a monthly parking spot. Since these **parking areas are so few and far between** and the demand is extremely high, the owners can charge up to 300 bucks a month! It's crazy, but every year the spots are gone as soon as school starts. Try to contact them in early summer to ensure a spot."

Q "**There is always Kirkwood, Radnor, Beacon Street (for most of the day)**. Also, there are other random avenues around campus that permit parking, although these spots go super fast each day."

Q "**Students generally cannot have cars on campus.** Those students who can have cars are in the School of Education or the School of Nursing because they have to travel to get to the schools and hospitals at which they work. However, I had a car this past semester and it was more of a hassle than it was worth. Boston is the craziest city ever to drive in, and I was too scared to go very far. No one has cars anyhow and it's not a problem because of public transportation."

Q "Honestly, parking on campus is a hassle. **It's very limited**. I wouldn't recommend bringing a car. Parking in Boston itself is annoying, and it's easy to get around Boston with the T, so I really don't think you need one."

Q "Parking is very difficult. You cannot park on campus unless you are a junior or a senior and are in the School of Education or the School of Nursing. **There are places to rent around campus for $100 to $150 a month**. You can park in the surrounding areas for free but you have to make sure you know all the restrictions so you don't get tickets. I lucked-out and was able to park for free at a family's house near campus since I baby-sat for them."

Q "**You can't bring a car until junior year**, which is the case at a lot of schools. It's kind of annoying because you can't drive home during breaks unless you get a ride with someone else, but I always take a shuttle plane home (you can buy a student package and they're pretty cheap). Plus, you really don't need a car when you live so close to a city. There's plenty of transportation on and off campus."

Q "Parking is very limited and mostly for nursing and teaching students. If you're lucky and you have a good reason to get a parking permit from student services, then you can park on campus but it's pretty expensive. **Parking off campus is difficult, too**, but a lot of my friends have cars off campus anyways. You just have to know when they don't ticket and move your car before they do, or you can buy a spot off campus for parking. You don't need a car, though; Boston has good public transportation."

Q "Students are not encouraged to have a car on campus; **there just isn't enough space**. However, junior year if you're a commuter student or senior year if you have an internship, you may apply for a parking permit, for which you still must pay. This situation really isn't a problem as BC is quite accessible by the T, by cab and by bus."

Q "It's not easy to park on campus and **I would not recommend bringing a car**; a car is more of a pain than it's worth. I had one for a semester."

The College Prowler Take On...
Parking

Parking is pretty much non-existent on campus! Nobody has cars, because BC really doesn't let anyone have a permit unless they are a student nurse or teacher. Some students choose to find local businesses where you can pay for parking, but that can run up to 200 bucks a month. It's really not worth bringing your car to campus. It's such a hassle and you probably won't need it that often anyway. No matter what, you will not be able to drive to class. If you do find a parking space, you'll probably want to leave your car there as long as you can because you're so unlikely to find another space. What's the point of bringing a car to campus just to leave it parked all the time?

Finding random spots in Brighton forces you to practically memorize the city parking restrictions and the timing of towing. Furthermore, parking on the streets surrounding Chestnut Hill is a royal pain, so if you are lucky enough to have your own car, it's easier to just leave it at home with your folks. Plus, public transportation is good enough to get you where you're going, and honestly, driving is crazy here anyway. The T and BC buses are much easier and cheaper.

The College Prowler® Grade on

Parking: D-

A high grade in this section indicates that parking is both available and affordable, and that parking enforcement isn't overly severe.

The Lowdown On...
Transportation

Ways to Get Around Town:

On Campus
The BC Bus, which runs weekdays from 8 a.m.–12 a.m. in Boston and 8 a.m.–6 p.m. around Newton.

Public Transportation
MBTA, which runs until 2 a.m.

Taxi Cabs
City Cab (617) 536-5100
Red Cab (617) 623-4200
Veteran's (508) 673-5843

Car Rentals
Alamo
Local: (412) 472-5060
National: (800) 327-9633
www.alamo.com

Avis
Local: (412) 472-5200
National: (800) 831-2847
www.avis.com

Budget
Local: (412) 472-5252
National: (800) 527-0700
www.budget.com

Dollar
Local: (412) 472-5100
National: (800) 800-4000
www.dollar.com

➔

(Car rentals, continued)

Enterprise
Local: (412) 472-3490
National: (800) 736-8222
www.enterprise.com

Best Ways to Get Around Town

Red Cab

Veteran's Taxi (You can use Eagle bucks to pay for fare on Veteran's.)

Ways to Get Out of Town:

Airlines Serving Boston

Air Canada/Air Canada Jazz
(888) 247-2262
www.aircanada.ca

American
(800) 433-7300
www.aa.com

American Eagle
(800) 433-7300
www.aa.com

British Airways
(800) 247-9297
www.british-airways.com

Cape Air
(800) 352-0714
www.flycapeair.com

Continental
(800) 525-0280
www.continental.com

Delta Air Lines
(800) 221-1212
www.delta.com

Northwest
(800) 225-2525
www.nwa.com

(Airlines, continued)

United
(800) 241-6522
www.ual.com

US Airways
(800) 428-4322
www.usairways.com

Airport

Logan International Airport, (617) 567-7844. The airport is approximately 20 minutes driving from Boston College.

How to Get to the Airport

MBTA (Blue Line), or Ted Williams Tunnel

A cab ride to the airport costs about $30

Greyhound and Amtrak

It's easy to take the T to the Greyhound or Amtrak station. For more information, check out their Web sites at *www.greyhound.com* and *www.amtrak.com*.

Travel Agents

Boston Travel Agency

227 Hanover Street

Boston, MA

(617) 227-9697

For people at BC, there is also STS Travel, which is on campus in the basement of Carney Hall.

Students Speak Out On...
Transportation

"People take the T and cabs everywhere they go, and you walk whenever you're on campus. Boston is pretty much a walking city, but you'll get used to it after a while."

Q "The T is really convenient. The green line starts right at the BC campus, but depending on where you're going, it could take forever to get there. Cabs are everywhere, too, but they're really pricey."

Q "Public transportation is quite convenient. The T line, which is the above-ground tram service, **has a line that goes directly to the foot of lower campus**. In addition to that, BC runs shuttle buses up and down Commonwealth Avenue for off-campus students, and also to bring students to the D line which goes straight into town. There are airport shuttle services and we are fairly close to the train station as well."

Q "Public transportation is very easy to use. Our campus has access to three different T lines that run to different parts of the city, access to a shuttle bus, and access to other public transportation buses. **It usually costs around a dollar to use the public transportation system**."

Q "**The T is great**. You'll get anywhere you need to get as long as it's before the T shuts down, which is at like 1 or 2 a.m., depending on your location. Then it's about a $15 or $25 cab ride. Always go with friends, it's cheaper. Just be careful not to get kicked off. I know people who have been arrested for acting like total jerks!"

Q "BC buses are semi-reliable and run to the Newton campus and to Cleveland circle. **Public buses are also easy to use**. For example, the 86 will take you to Harvard Square in about 20 minutes, instead of taking the hour-long T ride."

Q "**Public transportation is a breeze**. It's easy and convenient, but awfully slow."

Q "**The last stop on the T is at BC**, so it's extremely easy to go in and out of the city."

The College Prowler Take On...
Transportation

The public transportation system consists of the T, Boston's version of a subway, and the BC bus. The BC bus can go either to Newton or to Cleveland Circle, where restaurants, a few bars, and pharmacies are located. It can be quicker than the T, depending on where you are going. It also depends on the time of day.

The T will take you pretty much anywhere in Boston, but it is not the quickest subway ever invented. It can be a long day if you decide to take the T from BC to downtown, but for shorter rides at off-peak times, the T is the way to go. Most T fares cost one dollar, and the T shuts down after 2 a.m. Still, while it is working, it's the cheapest way to get around town. There is a nighttime bus system, the "Night Owl," which runs a similar route to the T, but few students utilize the bus. Cabs are common and convenient. After all, they just take you right to your door instead of having to wait at some bus stop or T stop. They can also be somewhat cheap if you and a whole bunch of friends cram into them, but try to use them only for nights out and rely on the T during the day.

B+

The College Prowler® Grade on
Transportation: B+

A high grade for Transportation indicates that campus buses, public buses, cabs, and rental cars are readily-available and affordable. Other determining factors include proximity to an airport and the necessity of transportation.

Weather

The Lowdown On...
Weather

Average Temperature:

Fall:	59 °F
Winter:	35 °F
Spring:	60 °F
Summer:	75 °F

Average Precipitation:

Fall:	3.43 in.
Winter:	3.99 in.
Spring:	3.60 in.
Summer:	3.06 in.

Students Speak Out On...
Weather

> **"It's Boston. We get all four seasons here, but our weather is a little wacky these days. For the most part, it is cold in winter with snow and ice and warm in summer. It is mild in the fall and spring, with rain and both cool and warm days."**

Q "The majority of the school year is spent shivering on your way to class, as **the winter is just brutal in Boston**. Yet when the hot weather comes around in late April, it's the absolute best feeling!"

Q "You definitely get four solid seasons at Boston College. **Autumn is absolutely gorgeous with the surrounding trees all changing colors**. Try to take a day-trip to New Hampshire or Vermont to see some more of the area's foliage. The winter is rough, but the spring is just beautiful, when we have a spring, that is!"

Q "I have **never felt as cold in my life** as I did when I stepped off the plane in Boston after Christmas break. It's shocking."

Q "New England weather is an acquired taste. You can find yourself wearing shorts in December and an Irish-knit sweater in June. Boston's climate is the most unpredictable and ludicrous phenomenon of Mother Nature, but please don't let it deter your from coming to our beautiful campus. **Bring any article of clothing you've ever owned**, and plan on buying more when you get here. It's just that silly."

Q "**The first few weeks of school are usually really warm**, and the dorms can get super sticky. The real winter doesn't begin until second semester and it lasts until about April. Then it can be a mixed bag from freezing rain to 90 degree days. It's totally unpredictable!"

Q "It starts to get cold in late October, **doesn't really snow much until January and February**, warms up in March, and then everyone is wearing skirts and shorts and laying out by the time finals come around in May."

Q "My roommate was from Detroit and handled the weather easily. **Coming from Atlanta, I found it really cold**, but nothing a ski jacket couldn't fix."

Q "I'm from Long Island, New York, so the weather was pretty much the same for me except a little colder. **It's beautiful in the summer and spring**, and in the fall, it's amazing when the trees change colors. The winter is a bit too cold for me. This winter was very mild, though, and we have a three week break from December to January so we didn't have to be there for the really cold part of winter."

Q "**It's New England and that means it's cold here**. It also snows. I hate snow, but I still love going to school here, and when it's really bad out classes are cancelled. This year has been weird, but you will find more sun than rain, and the Cape has prime beach weather for many months."

Q "The weather is decent. **It's incredibly warm in September, but then it's all downhill from there**. It gets cold and windy, but it's definitely doable. Generally the winters aren't too bad, and you get used to it."

Q "**The weather is different all day long**. In one day, it will range from 30 degrees to 80 degrees. Boston has the craziest weather."

The College Prowler Take On...
Weather

The weather in Boston can run the extremes. Seasons don't seem to matter too much here either. The weather can change drastically during the course of a day, and sometimes just during the hour you're in class. You might even find yourself wearing winter clothes in summer and summer clothes in winter. It truly is unpredictable here, but you do get used to it. Usually the fall is absolutely gorgeous and you only need a light jacket and fleece. However, the winter is freakishly brutal and sweaters, coats, hats and gloves are necessities. Snow can pile up, and classes just won't cancel unless it's really, really treacherous out. Make sure you bring boots or at least shoes that are good in the snow.

Spring (if Mother Nature is kind enough to give you one) lasts about two or three weeks during second semester, and that's when all the short skirts and flip-flops come out. Heat waves are known to prevail during finals, so quality studying becomes an arduous endeavor. All in all, the weather at BC will give you a good variety of everything you could want from Mother Nature. You just might get it at unexpected times. Bring clothes and supplies for all seasons, and it probably wouldn't hurt to carry a sweater and umbrella with you at all times, just in case.

C-

The College Prowler® Grade on
Weather: C-

A high Weather grade designates that temperatures are mild and rarely reach extremes, that the campus tends to be sunny rather than rainy, and that weather is fairly consistent rather than unpredictable.

Report Card Summary

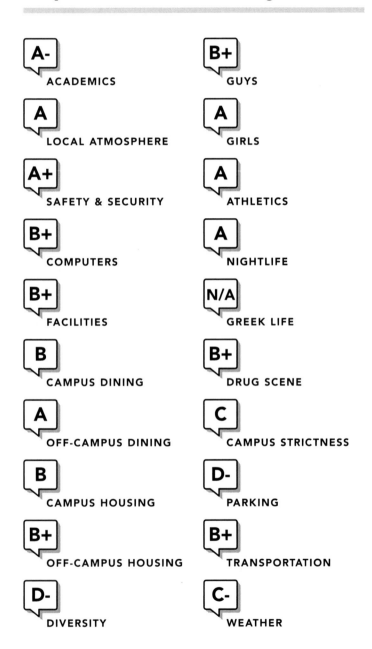

A- ACADEMICS

A LOCAL ATMOSPHERE

A+ SAFETY & SECURITY

B+ COMPUTERS

B+ FACILITIES

B CAMPUS DINING

A OFF-CAMPUS DINING

B CAMPUS HOUSING

B+ OFF-CAMPUS HOUSING

D- DIVERSITY

B+ GUYS

A GIRLS

A ATHLETICS

A NIGHTLIFE

N/A GREEK LIFE

B+ DRUG SCENE

C CAMPUS STRICTNESS

D- PARKING

B+ TRANSPORTATION

C- WEATHER

Overall Experience

Students Speak Out On...
Overall Experience

{ "I had an incredible four years. I took some wonderful classes, made several amazing friends, worked hard, and had plenty of fun. I wish, though, that I had been more promiscuous."

Q "There are times when I wish I went somewhere more diverse, or to a smaller liberal arts school, but for the most part I've had a really great time and I've met some wonderful people. So, **if I could go back in time, I wouldn't change anything**."

Q "I love BC. There are obvious downsides that may tip the scales a different way for you in making your decision, but **I think that BC is the place I was meant to be**. I'm so happy here. I would never think of transferring."

Q "Overall it's a good school as long as you meet the right people. I've had a hard time finding people that I click with, so my experience hasn't been as good as that of others. But **if you meet fun people, it's the best**; awesome academics, great career possibilities upon graduating, fun places and parties to go to. Just make sure you get a group of friends that you can imagine yourself liking for four years."

Q "As a recent BC grad, the only place that I wish I were now is back there. The connections and relationships that you form while at a school like BC define the greatness that the university embodies. Unlike most schools in this country, **your BC experience does not end after graduation**. It follows you in everything you do, in every town or city you find yourself in. There will always be a BC grad looking to help you out, wanting to talk about how the campus is changing and what the football team's schedule looks like. It's a sensation that is unparalleled, and something that will truly make you proud to say that you graduated from Boston College."

Q "**Boston College was a great experience**, if I wished I had gone somewhere else, I wouldn't be going back for grad school."

Q "I loved BC. **I had some good and bad experiences**, but overall I'm glad I came to BC and made the friends that I did. I'm sure you'll have a good experience too if you choose BC. It just depends on what you make of it and on the friends that you make. Just join a lot of activities and study hard, but remember to have fun, too."

Q "I have had the best two years so far at BC. I absolutely love it here. **The teachers are great and the classes are very interesting**. The city has offered so many opportunities. I'm glad I'm here and I don't want to be anywhere else."

Q **"I don't think I'd be this happy anywhere else.**
I absolutely love BC. I'm not just trying to sell the school
to you, because, really what would I get from that? I'm
just telling you how I feel and there are probably a lot of
people at BC that don't like it as much as I do. All I
know is that out of all of my friends from home that
went away to school, I am the happiest and having the
best time away."

Q "Honestly, I am having a good time at school because
I found a really nice group of friends freshman year."

The College Prowler Take On...
Overall Experience

The general feeling seems to be that Boston College is a wonderful school and an incredible experience. However, the first few years can be tough, as you may not be prepared for the enormity of the college experience. If you're from a very diverse high school, you will certainly be shocked at the very different atmosphere that will surround you at BC. Furthermore, so many of your peers can appear like they're having the time of their lives, and you might feel like you're faking it, especially at first. Yet, staying the course is absolutely worth it, as Boston College is a wonderful institution with many dynamic people that will truly challenge and amaze you. If you give the school a little time to grow on you, it certainly will and you'll be really glad you gave it a chance.

Also keep in mind that while parties and tailgates are enjoyable, they are not the only things college life is about. Yes, you want to have fun, and you will once you get to know people a little better, but there are other reasons you came here. Remember that you are going to college to receive an exceptional college education, and Boston College will certainly deliver that and then some. Friendships flourish, enriching academics abound, and you'll walk away a changed person.

The Inside Scoop

The Lowdown On...
The Inside Scoop

Tips to Succeed at BC

• Expand your friendship circles! Just because people live in your hall doesn't mean there aren't thousands of other very cool individuals to form relationships with.

• "Study hard, play hard," actually does work.

• Go away for spring break, either on service trips or somewhere tropical. You can see your hometown friends during the summer.

• Always check the PEPS before class selection.

Things I Wish I Knew Before Coming to BC

It doesn't always click right away for everyone. Give yourself time to adjust if you don't fall in love with Boston College during the first week. Don't think you should instantaneously feel at home.

School Spirit

Students at BC have a lot of pride in their school. Come to a football game, and you'll see what I mean.

Traditions

Most of our traditions center around sports. Students at BC go to games to cheer for their team. They tailgate before and party after. They also know every word of the fight song.

Finding a Job or Internship

The Lowdown On...
Finding a Job or Internship

Career Center

Southwell Hall
38 Commonwealth Avenue
Chestnut Hill, MA 02467
(617) 552-3430
careerc@bc.edu
www.bc.edu/offices/careers

The Career Center is extremely helpful and contains many resources for you at every point in your college career, from choosing a major, to picking a grad school, or looking for your first real job.

Advice

If you are uncertain about anything, go talk to the Career Center. They'll help you find the job or internship that's right for you. Also, don't think you're too young for career advice. Even freshmen could benefit from talking to them and making sure they're on the right path to get them where they want to be in the future.

Career Center Resources & Services

Internship placement

Job advice

Help choosing a major

Grad school advising

Interview skills

Resume writing

Alumni

The Lowdown On...
Alumni

Web Site:

www.bc.edu/friends/alumni/community

Office:

Boston College Alumni Association
825 Centre Street
Newton, MA 02458-2527
(800) 669-8430
alumni.comments@bc.edu

Services Available:

E-mail forwarding

Boston College graduates are your most valuable resource for establishing a career network, which is why the BC Alumni Career Network is so invaluable. These alumni have volunteered to provide career information, but not actual jobs. In short, you can ask them any career-related question except, "Can I have a job?" But their advice can be helpful.

➜

The Alumni House

The Alumni House is located on Center Street in Newton Campus. It is home to the Boston College Alumni Association.

Alumni Welcome Center

The Alumni Welcome Center is located on the first floor of Vanderslice Hall. It is another place that alumni can gather or go for more information on campus.

Major Alumni Events

Reunion Weekend – It's your typical reunion with everyone getting together to catch up. There's also dinner and presentations on how the school has changed and what it's like now.

Alumni Evening at the Arts Festival – This is a chance for alumni to get together and listen to some good music and catch up.

Alumni Publications

Boston College Magazine comes out four times a year.

Did You Know?

Famous BC Alums:

Doug Flutie (Class of 1985) – Former NFL quarterback, BC legend

Matt Hasselbeck (Class of 1997) – NFL quarterback

Jack Kerouac (Class of 1943) – Beat poet

John Kerry (JD, 1976) – Former Democratic candidate for President of the United States

Leonard Nimoy (Class of 1952) – *Star Trek* actor

Chris O'Donnell (Class of 1992) – Actor

Student Organizations

There are more than 400 student organizations on campus. The following is a partial list:

Accounting Academy, Boston College

ACM, Student Chapter of the

Acoustics, Boston College

Against the Current

AHANA Graduate Student Association

Allies of Boston College

Animal Rights Organization

Another Choice on Campus

Appalachia Volunteers, Boston College

Armenian Club of Boston College

Army ROTC, Boston College

Artplosion

Asia Business Society

Asian Baptist Student Koinonia (ABSK)

Asian Caucus

Asinine - Sketch & Improv Comedy

Bellarmine Pre-Law Council

Best Buddies at Boston College

Black Campus Ministry

Black Law Students Association (BLSA)

Black Student Forum

Board of Student Advisors - Law School

Brazilian Club of Boston College

Campus School Volunteers of Boston College

Cape Verdean Student Association of Boston College

Caribbean Culture Club

Casa Hispánica

Cheerleading, Boston College

Chi Alpha Christian Fellowship

Chinese Students Association

Chorale, University

Christian Legal Society, BC Law School

Circle K, Boston College

College Republicans of Boston College

Committee for Creative Enactments

Crew, Boston College

Cycling Club, Boston College

Dance Ensemble, Boston College

Dance Organization of Boston College

Democrats, Boston College

Domestic Violence Advocacy Program

Dramatics Society, The Boston College

Dynamics, The Boston College

Eagle EMS

Elements - undergraduate research journal

English Department Graduate Colloquium

Entrepreneur Society, Boston College

Environmental Action Coalition

Environmental Law Society - ELS

Federalist Society, BC Law School Chapter

Finance Academy, Boston College

Four Boston (4Boston)

Fulton Debating Society

Golden Key International Honour Society

Hello . . . Shovelhead! Sketch Comedy

Hillel

India Club

Information Technology Club, Boston College

Intellectual Property and Technology Forum, Law School

International Law Society

Intervarsity Christian Fellowship

Invest 'n Kids

Investment Club, Boston College

Irish Society, Boston College

Japan Club of Boston College

Jewish Law Students Association

Just Art

Karate Club, Boston College

Korean Student Association, Boston College

La Maison Francaise

Lambda Law Students Association

Latin American Law Students Association

Law Running Club

Law School Veterans Association, Boston College (BCLSVA)

Law Students Association

Marathon Team, Campus School Volunteers of BC

Marketing Academy

Mathematics Society, Boston College

MBA Healthcare Club

Minority Association of Pre-Health Students, Boston College (MAPS)

Mock Trial Program, Boston College

Model United Nations

Naked Singularity

National Lawyers Guild

O'Connell House

Older Law Students Organization

Organization of Latin American Affairs (OLAA)

Partnership for Life

Peer Education Network

Political Science Association, Boston College

Public Interest Law Foundation (PILF)

Republicans, Boston College

Role Players and Strategy Enthusiasts (RPSE)

Romance Languages Graduate Association (RLGA)

ROTC (Army) at Boston College

Rugby Football Club Boston College

Saint Thomas More Society of Boston College

Salt & Light Company

School of Management Student Government (SOMG)

Ski and Snowboard Club, Boston College

Soccer, Boston College Club

South Asian Students Association (SASA)

Southeast Asian Students Association (SEASA)

Student Agencies, Boston College

Student Organization Funding Committee

Students for Corporate Citizenship

Students in Free Enterprise (SIFE)

Stylus

Sub Turri

Swing Kids

UGBC - Undergraduate Government of Boston College

UGBC Senate

United in Christ

Vietnamese Student Association at Boston College

Women's Law Center

WZBC Radio - FM 90.3

The Best & Worst

The Ten BEST Things About Boston College

1	Gorgeous campus
2	Excellent education
3	Awesome athletics
4	Knowledgeable professors
5	Jesuit teaching
6	Beautiful people
7	Incredible atmosphere
8	Major history and tradition
9	New dorms
10	Senior week!

The Ten **WORST** Things About Boston College

1 Minimal diversity

2 Depressing weather

3 Bad jeans on guys

4 Newton residents can be depressing

5 Conceited, arrogant teaching

6 Some dorms could use a makeover (Edmonds)

7 Overly-selective volunteer organizations

8 The BCPD are strict

9 Rude and unwelcoming administration

10 Moving in and out of dorms

Visiting

The Lowdown On...
Visiting

Hotel Information:

Best Western Terrace Inn
1650 Commonwealth Ave,
Brighton, MA 02135
(617) 566-6260
www.bostonbw.com
Distance from Campus: 1 mile
Price Rance: $150–$200

Courtyard by Marriott, Brookline
40 Webster Street, Brookline,
MA 02446
(617) 743-1393
(800) 321-2211
www.marriott.com/BOSBL
Distance from Campus: 2 miles
Price Rance: $200–$250

→

Holiday Inn Brookline
1200 Beacon Street, Brookline
(617) 277-1200
(800) HOLIDAY
Distance from Campus: 2 miles
Price Rance: $175–$225

Holiday Inn Newton
399 Grove Street, Newton
(617) 969-5300
(800) HOLIDAY
Distance from Campus: 3 miles
Price Rance: $125–$175

Marriott Newton
2345 Commonwealth Ave.,
Newton
(617) 969-1000
(800) 228-9290
Distance from Campus: 5 miles
Price Rance: $125–$150

Sheraton Needham Hotel
100 Cabot Street, Needham
781-444-1110
(800) 325-3535
Distance from Campus: 4 miles
Price Rance: $150–$200

Directions to Campus

Boston College is located in the Chestnut Hill section of Newton, Massachusetts. The campus is approximately six miles west of the city of Boston.

From the North and South

Take Interstate 95 (Route 128) to Exit 24 (Route 30). Proceed east on Route 30, also known as Commonwealth Avenue, and follow for about five miles to Boston College.

From the West

Take the Massachusetts Turnpike (Route 90) to Exit 17. At the first set of lights after the exit ramp, take a right onto Centre Street. Follow Centre Street to the fourth set of lights, and turn left onto Commonwealth Avenue. Follow Commonwealth Avenue 1.5 miles to Boston College.

From Downtown Boston

Take the Massachusetts Turnpike (Route 90) to Exit 17. Take a left over the bridge after passing the Sheraton Tara Hotel. Take the first right onto Centre Street. Follow above directions from Centre Street.

Public Transportation

The Boston College branch of the MBTA's "Green Line" (B) ends at the Boston-Newton boundary on Commonwealth Avenue. Cross the street and walk by St. Ignatius Church and follow the perimeter road around to campus entrances.

Words to Know

Academic Probation – A suspension imposed on a student if he or she fails to keep up with the school's minimum academic requirements. Those unable to improve their grades after receiving this warning can face dismissal.

Beer Pong/Beirut – A drinking game involving cups of beer arranged in a pyramid shape on each side of a table. The goal is to get a ping pong ball into one of the opponent's cups by throwing the ball or hitting it with a paddle. If the ball lands in a cup, the opponent is required to drink the beer.

Bid – An invitation from a fraternity or sorority to 'pledge' (join) that specific house.

Blue-Light Phone – Brightly-colored phone posts with a blue light bulb on top. These phones exist for security purposes and are located at various outside locations around most campuses. In an emergency, a student can pick up one of these phones (free of charge) to connect with campus police or a security escort.

Campus Police – Police who are specifically assigned to a given institution. Campus police are typically not regular city officers; they are employed by the university in a full-time capacity.

Club Sports – A level of sports that falls somewhere between varsity and intramural. If a student is unable to commit to a varsity team but has a lot of passion for athletics, a club sport could be a better, less intense option. Even less demanding, intramural (IM) sports often involve no traveling and considerably less time.

Cocaine – An illegal drug. Also known as "coke" or "blow," cocaine often resembles a white crystalline or powdery substance. It is highly addictive and dangerous.

Common Application – An application with which students can apply to multiple schools.

Course Registration – The period of official class selection for the upcoming quarter or semester. Prior to registration, it is best to prepare several back-up courses in case a particular class becomes full. If a course is full, students can place themselves on the waitlist, although this still does not guarantee entry.

Division Athletics – Athletic classifications range from Division I to Division III. Division IA is the most competitive, while Division III is considered to be the least competitive.

Dorm – A dorm (or dormitory) is an on-campus housing facility. Dorms can provide a range of options from suite-style rooms to more communal options that include shared bathrooms. Most first-year students live in dorms. Some upperclassmen who wish to stay on campus also choose this option.

Early Action – An application option with which a student can apply to a school and receive an early acceptance response without a binding commitment. This system is becoming less and less available.

Early Decision – An application option that students should use only if they are certain they plan to attend the school in question. If a student applies using the early decision option and is admitted, he or she is required and bound to attend that university. Admission rates are usually higher among students who apply through early decision, as the student is clearly indicating that the school is his or her first choice.

Ecstasy – An illegal drug. Also known as "E" or "X," ecstasy looks like a pill and most resembles an aspirin. Considered a party drug, ecstasy is very dangerous and can be deadly.

Ethernet – An extremely fast Internet connection available in most university-owned residence halls. To use an Ethernet connection properly, a student will need a network card and cable for his or her computer.

Fake ID – A counterfeit identification card that contains false information. Most commonly, students get fake IDs with altered birthdates so that they appear to be older than 21 (and therefore of legal drinking age). Even though it is illegal, many college students have fake IDs in hopes of purchasing alcohol or getting into bars.

Frosh – Slang for "freshman" or "freshmen."

Hazing – Initiation rituals administered by some fraternities or sororities as part of the pledging process. Many universities have outlawed hazing due to its degrading, and sometimes dangerous, nature.

Intramurals (IMs) – A popular, and usually free, sport league in which students create teams and compete against one another. These sports vary in competitiveness and can include a range of activities—everything from billiards to water polo. IM sports are a great way to meet people with similar interests.

Keg – Officially called a half-barrel, a keg contains roughly 200 12-ounce servings of beer.

LSD – An illegal drug, also known as acid, this hallucinogenic drug most commonly resembles a tab of paper.

Marijuana – An illegal drug, also known as weed or pot; along with alcohol, marijuana is one of the most commonly-found drugs on campuses across the country.

Major –The focal point of a student's college studies; a specific topic that is studied for a degree. Examples of majors include physics, English, history, computer science, economics, business, and music. Many students decide on a specific major before arriving on campus, while others are simply "undecided" until declaring a major. Those who are extremely interested in two areas can also choose to double major.

Meal Block – The equivalent of one meal. Students on a meal plan usually receive a fixed number of meals per week. Each meal, or "block," can be redeemed at the school's dining facilities in place of cash. Often, a student's weekly allotment of meal blocks will be forfeited if not used.

Minor – An additional focal point in a student's education. Often serving as a complement or addition to a student's main area of focus, a minor has fewer requirements and prerequisites to fulfill than a major. Minors are not required for graduation from most schools; however some students who want to explore many different interests choose to pursue both a major and a minor.

Mushrooms – An illegal drug. Also known as "'shrooms," this drug resembles regular mushrooms but is extremely hallucinogenic.

Off-Campus Housing – Housing from a particular landlord or rental group that is not affiliated with the university. Depending on the college, off-campus housing can range from extremely popular to non-existent. Students who choose to live off campus are typically given more freedom, but they also have to deal with possible subletting scenarios, furniture, bills, and other issues. In addition to these factors, rental prices and distance often affect a student's decision to move off campus.

Office Hours – Time that teachers set aside for students who have questions about coursework. Office hours are a good forum for students to go over any problems and to show interest in the subject material.

Pledging – The early phase of joining a fraternity or sorority, pledging takes place after a student has gone through rush and received a bid. Pledging usually lasts between one and two semesters. Once the pledging period is complete and a particular student has done everything that is required to become a member, that student is considered a brother or sister. If a fraternity or a sorority would decide to "haze" a group of students, this initiation would take place during the pledging period.

Private Institution – A school that does not use tax revenue to subsidize education costs. Private schools typically cost more than public schools and are usually smaller.

Prof – Slang for "professor."

Public Institution – A school that uses tax revenue to subsidize education costs. Public schools are often a good value for in-state residents and tend to be larger than most private colleges.

Quarter System (or Trimester System) – A type of academic calendar system. In this setup, students take classes for three academic periods. The first quarter usually starts in late September or early October and concludes right before Christmas. The second quarter usually starts around early to mid–January and finishes up around March or April. The last academic quarter, or "third quarter," usually starts in late March or early April and finishes up in late May or Mid-June. The fourth quarter is summer. The major difference between the quarter system and semester system is that students take more, less comprehensive courses under the quarter calendar.

RA (Resident Assistant) – A student leader who is assigned to a particular floor in a dormitory in order to help to the other students who live there. An RA's duties include ensuring student safety and providing assistance wherever possible.

Recitation – An extension of a specific course; a review session. Some classes, particularly large lectures, are supplemented with mandatory recitation sessions that provide a relatively personal class setting.

Rolling Admissions – A form of admissions. Most commonly found at public institutions, schools with this type of policy continue to accept students throughout the year until their class sizes are met. For example, some schools begin accepting students as early as December and will continue to do so until April or May.

Room and Board – This figure is typically the combined cost of a university-owned room and a meal plan.

Room Draw/Housing Lottery – A common way to pick on-campus room assignments for the following year. If a student decides to remain in university-owned housing, he or she is assigned a unique number that, along with seniority, is used to determine his or her housing for the next year.

Rush – The period in which students can meet the brothers and sisters of a particular chapter and find out if a given fraternity or sorority is right for them. Rushing a fraternity or a sorority is not a requirement at any school. The goal of rush is to give students who are serious about pledging a feel for what to expect.

Semester System – The most common type of academic calendar system at college campuses. This setup typically includes two semesters in a given school year. The fall semester starts around the end of August or early September and concludes before winter vacation. The spring semester usually starts in mid-January and ends in late April or May.

Student Center/Rec Center/Student Union – A common area on campus that often contains study areas, recreation facilities, and eateries. This building is often a good place to meet up with fellow students; depending on the school, the student center can have a huge role or a non-existent role in campus life.

Student ID – A university-issued photo ID that serves as a student's key to school-related functions. Some schools require students to show these cards in order to get into dorms, libraries, cafeterias, and other facilities. In addition to storing meal plan information, in some cases, a student ID can actually work as a debit card and allow students to purchase things from bookstores or local shops.

Suite – A type of dorm room. Unlike dorms that feature communal bathrooms shared by the entire floor, suites offer bathrooms shared only among the suite. Suite-style dorm rooms can house anywhere from two to ten students.

TA (Teacher's Assistant) – An undergraduate or grad student who helps in some manner with a specific course. In some cases, a TA will teach a class, assist a professor, grade assignments, or conduct office hours.

Undergraduate – A student in the process of studying for his or her bachelor's degree.

California Colleges

California dreamin'?
This book is a must have for you!

CALIFORNIA COLLEGES
7¼" X 10", 762 Pages Paperback
$29.95 Retail
1-59658-501-3

Stanford, UC Berkeley, Caltech—California is home to some of America's greatest institutes of higher learning. *California Colleges* gives the lowdown on 24 of the best, side by side, in one prodigious volume.

New England Colleges

Looking for peace in the Northeast?
Pick up this regional guide to New England!

NEW ENGLAND COLLEGES
7¼" X 10", 1015 Pages Paperback
$29.95 Retail
1-59658-504-8

New England is the birthplace of many prestigious universities, and with so many to choose from, picking the right school can be a tough decision. With inside information on over 34 competive Northeastern schools, *New England Colleges* provides the same high-quality information prospective students expect from College Prowler in one all-inclusive, easy-to-use reference.

Schools of the South

Headin' down south? This book will help you find your way to the perfect school!

SCHOOLS OF THE SOUTH
7¼" X 10", 773 Pages Paperback
$29.95 Retail
1-59658-503-X

Southern pride is always strong. Whether it's across town or across state, many Southern students are devoted to their home sweet home. *Schools of the South* offers an honest student perspective on 36 universities available south of the Mason-Dixon.

Untangling
the Ivy League

The ultimate book for everything Ivy!

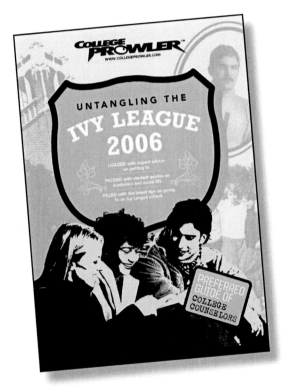

UNTANGLING THE IVY LEAGUE
7¼" X 10", 567 Pages Paperback
$24.95 Retail
1-59658-500-5

Ivy League students, alumni, admissions officers,
and other top insiders get together to tell it like it is.
Untangling the Ivy League covers every aspect—from
admissions and athletics to secret societies and urban
legends—of the nation's eight oldest, wealthiest, and
most competitive colleges and universities.

Need Help Paying For School?

Apply for our scholarship!

College Prowler awards thousands of dollars a year
to students who compose the best essays.
E-mail scholarship@collegeprowler.com for more
information, or call 1-800-290-2682.

Apply now at ***www.collegeprowler.com***

Tell Us What Life Is Really Like at Your School!

Have you ever wanted to let people know what your college is really like? Now's your chance to help millions of high school students choose the right college.

Let your voice be heard.

Check out **www.collegeprowler.com** for more info!

Need More Help?

Do you have more questions about this school? Can't find a certain statistic? College Prowler is here to help. We are the best source of college information out there. We have a network of thousands of students who can get the latest information on any school to you ASAP. E-mail us at info@collegeprowler.com with your college-related questions.

E-Mail Us Your College-Related Questions!

Check out ***www.collegeprowler.com*** for more details.
1-800-290-2682

Write For Us!
Get published! Voice your opinion.

Writing a College Prowler guidebook is both fun and rewarding; our open-ended format allows your own creativity free reign. Our writers have been featured in national newspapers and have seen their names in bookstores across the country. Now is your chance to break into the publishing industry with one of the country's fastest-growing publishers!

Apply now at ***www.collegeprowler.com***

Contact editor@collegeprowler.com or
call 1-800-290-2682 for more details.

Pros and Cons

Still can't figure out if this is the right school for you?
You've already read through this in-depth guide; why not
list the pros and cons? It will really help with narrowing down
your decision and determining whether or not
this school is right for you.

Pros	Cons
....	....
....	....
....	....
....	....
....	....
....	....
....	....
....	....
....	....
....	....
....	....
....	....
....	....